WINNING THE PROPERTY WAR

Winning the Property War

Doug Hopkins

Winning the Property War
ISBN-10: 097061540X
ISBN-13: 978-0-9706154-0-4

To my mom and dad

Contents

Foreword

I've always had big dreams for both of my children and they didn't let me down, but it seems that I didn't quite dream high enough for Doug, as he just keeps flying higher and higher. We are in the antique business, and in order to keep his interest as we dragged him from show to flea market to estate sale, we got him interested in baseball cards. It was there that he began to buy, sell and trade—a hobby that he has made a career out of. I remember getting a phone call from the principal of his elementary school telling me that instead of buying his lunch he was spending his lunch money buying baseball cards from his friends. When he graduated from sixth grade my dad gave him ten shares of stock, and he developed an interest in the stock market. Again, the buying and selling was his main interest. The next thing I knew he was in college and asking his father and me to send him to real estate school because he had decided he wanted to buy and sell houses. If I remember correctly, he bought his first house at the age of twenty-four. I helped him with the down payment—now he helps me out instead. From that time on he flourished, learning the business and buying more and more homes. I never in my wildest dreams thought that he'd fly so high, and still am stunned when people recognize him and stop him on the street. After all, he's my son—I forget that he's accomplished so much. I'm so proud of him, and enjoy watching him soar. I'm sure his grandfather knows and is just as proud.

—Mom

Introduction

This book is really a culmination of my life's work. How I did what I did and what events shaped me in the past. You won't find anything in this book that only a lucky few can do. You won't find methods that only someone with a hefty bank account can accomplish. And you don't have to travel all across the country in order to be successful as a real estate investor.

My book covers everything you need to know on how to start, build and run a successful enterprise. You can be as big or as small as you want, but either way the same principles apply. Everything this book covers I've done many, many times.

There's no reason for you, the reader, to try things on your own and make mistakes over and over again, decreasing your chances for success. I've already traveled those roads and made those mistakes or watched others make them. There's no reason for you to go it alone, because I've already been there.

It's sort of like a story of a guy and a girl who each independently decide to pick up the game of golf. Golf is big out here in Arizona and people from all over the world travel here in order to play the famous courses.

These two people—we'll call them Joe and Jill—decide to join the crowd and pick up the leisurely game of golf. After all, it will be good for their business to take clients out for a round, as well as enjoy some quality family time on the links. How hard can it be, right?

Those people on TV seem to be enjoying themselves as they compete against one another in a tournament. If the pros can get the ball on the green in three or four shots, surely anyone else can get there in five or six.

So Joe goes out to the sporting-goods store, which has a special department that measures Joe's height, swing, club speed and other important factors to design a custom set of clubs. After a few weeks his clubs arrive and he dons his brand-new golf gear and heads out to the driving range.

Jill goes to a store that specializes in golf and tennis, and she too goes through a measurement routine that can properly identify the perfect set of clubs based on various characteristics. The pro at the golf shop then orders Jill's clubs, and they arrive within a couple of weeks. She picks up her clubs, gets a complementary box of top-of-the-line golf balls and contacts the instructor at a driving range for her first lesson.

Joe grabs an extra-large bucket of range balls, the ones with the red stripe around them, and heads to the practice tee. He decides to pull out a five-iron. Placing a few golf balls on the mat, he swings away. His first swing, though, misses the ball entirely. On the second swing he makes contact, but the ball bounces a few hops in front of him.

He continues to practice, but he's not getting the balls to go where they're supposed to. Joe's no quitter, though. He realizes he's still a beginner and he's determined to get good at this game. Joe hits a full bucket of balls and replenishes his bucket for still another hour of practice. He's not going to leave the range today until he begins hitting the ball the way he wants to. Like the pros on TV do.

Jill makes her appointment with the golf instructor and begins her first lesson. The pro tells her what she can expect to learn and how long it will take her. She will also need to practice, but practice the right way, with the proper grip, foot placement, weight transfer and everything else she needs to learn. It's a lot to be aware of, but practice makes perfect. At least as perfect as you can get in a game of golf. She doesn't need to figure out the proper stroke—it's already been explained to her. The pro points out her mistakes, corrects them for her and watches as her game progresses.

Fast-forward six weeks. Joe is as diligent as he is determined. He's at the driving range three or four times a week, each time hitting two large buckets of balls. And while he's making better contact, his shots all spin out to the right and he's not getting the distance he's supposed to be getting.

He's thinking he got shafted with the custom clubs he bought, and complains to the sporting-goods store where he bought them, but that didn't do any good.

Jill is also at the driving range three or four times a week, but she's there with her instructor. She's being taught the right way to hit the golf ball. She doesn't have to go through the sort of "trial by fire" that Joe is putting himself through.

After six weeks, who do you think is the better golfer? Of course it's Jill.

If you use this golf analogy as you prepare for your real estate investment career, you'll realize that I have the experience to teach you what you need to know. I made my mistakes and I'll share some of them with you so you don't have to make them. Know here and now that by following the steps laid out in my book you'll achieve all you want to achieve.

Buying real estate can allow the average person to acquire tremendous wealth over the course of a lifetime, but it's not the type of purchase that you can return within a few days after a bad case of buyer's remorse. You can't bring your sales receipt to the seller and ask for your money back. Once you sign that sales contract and put your signature on the closing documents, it's yours. But you won't have to be concerned about what to do with a property once you've acquired it, because buying it is just part of the process.

You will know in advance what to do with your real estate before you ever make an offer because you'll understand how to evaluate a prospective purchase. If it doesn't make the grade, you don't buy it. It really is that simple.

Becoming a real estate investor means just that—you're an investor. That's not to be redundant, but to point out that real estate shouldn't be speculative. It's not something that you need to bet on in order to make a profitable investment.

Real estate is a secure investment, but it's not very liquid. There should be no speculation when evaluating a purchase. It's not a gamble. There are millions of people who did gamble in the real estate industry in the last decade, and look what happened.

Let's take a closer look at what you will learn by reading these pages.

In the first chapter, you'll find out more about me. But, though I've bought more than ten thousand foreclosures, the story isn't about the numbers. No, the first chapter highlights the things that shaped me and motivated me to be where I am today. I'm no superstar. I'm not someone who is far better than anyone else or a know-it-all showing off what I've done. I'm a regular guy. I've made my share of mistakes in the past and am here today to tell you that if I can do it then anyone can.

I share the same basic skill sets that you have and you'll find out why I do the things I do and understand why I'm taking the time to help others achieve what I've achieved. If there's just one thing in this book that you should take away, it's the basic notion that *you can do this*. You really can.

This book contains no "get rich quick" schemes or wild-eyed promises about amassing millions in just a few short weeks. I wrote this book to help others, and if you're reading this now I'm honored and consider you a friend. I'll teach you what I know.

Chapter 2 reviews how we got to where we are today. The "Great Recession" didn't just affect homeowners in the United States; it was a financial tidal wave across the entire globe. Long-revered financial firms went bankrupt. Banks closed at a frightful rate and the federal government stepped in to save the financial industry.

In the early 2000s, a new breed of mortgage lenders hit the landscape. While there have always been mortgage companies that catered to borrowers with poor credit, the lending guidelines were relaxed like never before. Borrowers didn't have to have a job, good credit or even a down payment. "Liars' loans" was a common phrase referring to so-called "stated" documentation, in which the lender would use the information on the application without verifying it when approving a mortgage. A borrower could say he or she made a million dollars per month and the lender would use that figure to evaluate the loan.

Because more and more people were buying homes, home values increased at white-hot levels. Buyers would buy a home with no intention of paying back the mortgage, because it would be sold thirty days later at a higher price. Buyers could make a quick $20,000 or so on a "flip" with very little effort. Chapter 2 explores what happened during the foreclosure crisis, and why it will never happen again.

Chapter 3 highlights the foreclosure process. Banks and mortgage companies don't issue a loan with the intention of foreclosing on the property. A foreclosure means something dramatic has changed between the time the loan was approved and the time bank moves to take back the house. A foreclosure takes place in a judicial as well as a non-judicial state, and the differences are explained here.

This chapter also discusses how and when foreclosures take place, what happens when the borrower begins to miss payments and the legal rights of the homeowner and the lender.

Chapter 4 identifies where, when and how to find foreclosures. Lenders must follow a strict set of procedures when foreclosing and there are opportunities for investors at different stages of the foreclosure process.

Lenders can handle their own foreclosures in various ways, but they all want to avoid the foreclosure process if possible. If there is no other choice, they want to quickly sell the home and keep the property out of their inventory of real estate owned (REO) properties. There are many ways to find properties that can be purchased below market, including foreclosure services and bank websites.

Chapter 5 puts it all together and provides step-by-step instructions on how to buy and sell foreclosed property and other distressed real estate. You'll need financing, and we'll help identify the types of lenders you need to have at your disposal, from a traditional bank to a private lender.

This chapter explains how and where auctions are held, how to bid and what you can expect. Public records are an integral part of the foreclosure process and this chapter explains what they are, how to access them and how to take advantage of them.

In many cases you'll be able to physically inspect a property you hope to purchase, an important part of the evaluation process. But you'll also want to inspect the property's history by knowing how to order and interpret a preliminary title report and what you can learn from it.

Chapter 6 goes into detail on other ways to find and profit from real estate that may or may not be in the foreclosure process. The concept of real estate wholesaling is explained, with examples on how it works. You can find leads by using bandit signs. I explain how to build them and where to place them.

You can use the services of a "bird dog," or scout, to hunt down leads on your behalf. Successful marketing techniques and how to get your name out there are explained. There are a lot more places to find deals other than those listed in the public record.

Chapter 7 explains in detail the various financing options available to you, and how to decide which program is best for each individual situation.

Going beyond simple down-payment requirements, Chapter 7 highlights the various loan options you have, including loan terms, no-closing-cost loans and sources for down-payment funds you may have not thought of before, but that lenders accept every single day.

If you hold properties, you want to make sure they cash flow each month. Here you can find out what it's like to be a landlord and what you can expect when finding and evaluating prospective tenants.

While you will be your own boss, you also need to know how to surround yourself with helpful talent. Chapter 8 shows you who needs to be on your team and how they profit when you include them in your circle.

Being successful in the real estate industry means taking advantage of the skill sets of your peers. As well as gathering a solid team, you should seek out a coach or mentor. Someone you can go to when you have a question or want to bounce an idea off of a pro.

Chapter 9 will remind you that as you build your wealth you also want to protect it. The more properties you own the more vulnerable you may be regarding liability.

I'll talk about revocable and irrevocable trusts, LLCs, sole proprietorships and other legal business entities, along with the advantages and potential disadvantages of each. Without properly protecting your hard-earned assets, you might find you can lose them all if you're on the wrong end of a frivolous lawsuit.

The last chapter, Chapter 10, puts it all together. I'll tell you how I got started in my career and how to set up and run your own business. Everyone is a bit different, so not every business model works for everyone, but there are basic tenets in business management that you need to follow as you grow.

Whether you're building a mom-and-pop organization or a real estate office with more than a hundred agents working for you, there are steps along the way you need to take. But maybe you don't want to own a large real estate shop. Maybe you want to flip a couple of properties each year, and perhaps buy a rental or two. However you want to shape your future, you need to know how to set your goals, follow them and make adjustments along the way.

From designing a website to social-media techniques, this final chapter puts it all together for you.

I've also included at the back of the book an extensive glossary of terms that you'll encounter at some point in this business.

This is the only book that covers what you need to know from the very start to making your fortune in real estate investing. This book has been a pleasure to write, and I'm proud of it. I hope you'll have as much fun reading it as I did writing it.

Are you ready?

Then let's go!

CHAPTER 1
Who Is Doug Hopkins?

There's this kid I knew when I was growing up in Westchester County, New York. To most people, he appeared to be an ordinary kid. He minded his manners and helped his mom and dad in their business. He stayed out of trouble (for the most part).

Like most kids in the neighborhood, he walked to and from school each day. What was neat about this kid was that at young age he had the ability to recognize that people have needs, wants and desires. He realized that he could help people by fulfilling their needs.

True story. The elementary school he attended had a strict policy of no snacks or candy sold at the school. That's pretty much the rule today, but this school never had a concession stand or candy machine. His parents would give him money every day to buy his lunch at the school cafeteria. With his lunch money in his pocket, he would pass a little store every day on his way to school. One day he got an idea.

That morning he stopped by the store and bought lollipops and pieces of Bazooka bubblegum with the lunch money his parents gave him. He paid ten cents a lollipop and two cents for each piece of gum. You would think a young kid would eat his candy on the way to school. This kid had a better idea.

At school he sold one piece of gum for a dime and the lollipops for a quarter. He found eager buyers at school every day who would pay extra for some bubblegum or a sucker. He not only had enough money for lunch, but he made two or three dollars extra doing that every single day. Quite the entrepreneur, don't you think?

That kid was me.

And yes, my parents soon found out about my new venture. They were quite proud of me, as a matter of fact. My parents were antique dealers and they appreciated the notion of finding something at a bargain, fixing it up and then selling it for more. They traveled up and down the East Coast from my home in New York, attending antique shows and visiting dealerships. I not only got to tag along with them, but they also paid me to work for them.

If there was any one thing that shaped my early years it was watching my parents build their own business. I applied those same skills when I figured out how to buy candy and sell it to my schoolmates for a profit.

No, I didn't open up a savings account and put all my earnings in the bank. I was still a kid, and some of my profits went back to that very same store every day to buy a pack of baseball cards. I bought a pack of Topps baseball cards nearly every day and became quite the collector. I still enjoy collecting baseball memorabilia. Today my collection is worth a bundle.

Upstate New York at that time was really the perfect time and place to grow up. I was athletic, and played baseball and football. I had a pretty girlfriend and was very popular. I guess selling candy at school sort of helped on that front, right?

So how did I end up in Arizona? As with many things in life, it happened by accident. My parents' best friends, with whom our family was very close, moved to Arizona when I was still in grade school.

After they moved, we missed them greatly. New York to Arizona is quite a trip. They kept in touch and always wanted us to visit them during the winter. One year they invited us to spend Christmas with them. Back then, flying from New York to Arizona was very expensive and we just couldn't afford it. Or so we thought.

Then one day, as my mother was out browsing around antique stores, she found a painting that she liked, and she bought it. Normally, she would look for a good deal. Buy it and sell it for a profit in the store. She didn't buy this particular painting because of the low price, though; she bought it because she liked it. It was pretty, and she could visualize it hanging on the living room wall.

My dad saw the painting and thought it was a nice but, like with everything else, he wanted to have it appraised. When he did so, he found out that it was worth $25,000. That's right: $25,000! I forget the name of the artist, but what that painting really turned out to be was a trip to Arizona to spend Christmas with our friends.

I remember landing in Arizona in the middle of December and being blown away by its beauty. The sky was a clear blue with just a wisp of white clouds. The temperature was in the mid -seventies, a far cry from the ten degrees back in New York.

Driving to our friends' house I saw green like I'd never seen before. Though we were in a desert, they sure knew how to take care of a golf course. It was, to my eyes, the perfect place.

We enjoyed our stay, but soon had to return home to the cold New York winter. I constantly thought about Arizona and how nice the trip had been. I thanked my mom countless times for finding that painting and taking us.

Time went by and, without me knowing it, my parents were thinking of moving to Arizona and taking their antique business with them. As it happened, we did decide to move and made the long trip to Arizona. We got there in August. It was hot—*very* hot—and my memories of the pleasant December days were wiped out completely. This East Coast boy was about to experience a dramatic life change.

High School in the Desert

We moved to a city called Mesa, and I enrolled in school. But the school was much bigger than my old school back in New York. The entire population of my old high school was smaller than my new class in Arizona.

One might think the popular kid with the candy was outgoing, but in high school I was rather shy and this big new school quite frankly intimidated me. As all kids sometimes think, I thought no one liked me. I didn't bother to reach out to too many people, but then again no one reached out to me.

I was the kid who sat all by himself in the cafeteria. I had no friends and I missed my girlfriend and friends terribly. I was homesick. I wished my parents had never heard of Arizona. Back in New York I had been a popular kid who played sports and was the captain of the baseball team, but in Arizona I was a no-body.

I remember getting in trouble with my parents when I would sneak long-distance phone calls back to my girlfriend in New York. We would talk and talk and talk. The long-distance bill was in the hundreds of dollars.

Baseball tryouts were coming up and I thought that maybe if I could make the baseball team I could start making friends. So I tried out. My new high school turned out to be one of the top ranked schools in Arizona for athletics. The guys on this team had been playing together for years. I normally played catcher, and that's the position I tried out for. The returning catcher's name was Brian Banks. He went on to play professional ball with the Brewers. Needless to say, I didn't make the team.

I decided to try out for football. I was always athletic, and could play football well enough, but baseball was my sport. Although football wasn't my forte, I was big, and was hoping my size would get me on the team.

I tried out and I made it. When the fall season started and I attended practices, pretty soon making friends became easier. If you've played high school football you understand the bond that's created between the players and the coaches.

I had to overcome my shyness and get over the fact that I didn't make the baseball team, but I persevered. I made a lot of friends on the football team, and soon after that I quit making long-distance phone calls back home. Eventually I had more friends than I'd ever had before. It was easier at this school, simply because there were so many kids.

My "College" Days

High school was not very challenging for me academically. I was able to graduate with a high B average without much studying. I didn't get a scholarship, but I was college bound. When I enrolled, I wanted to have the full college experience, so I moved out of my parents' house and into the dorms. I was eager and ready to be an ASU student.

I realized very quickly that if I was absent the college did not notify my parents. Some teachers didn't even take attendance. Lacking accountability, I began studying the Nintendo arts and became the dorm videogame champion of Tecmo Football.

My school days felt like every day was a weekend. I was on my own for the first time in my life, and not handling it very well. My first semester grades came out, and I had a 2.0 GPA. Three C's, a B and a D. My parents, who were paying for my tuition, were not happy. I promised them I would do better my second semester. They told me if I couldn't maintain a B average they would not pay for my classes anymore.

My second semester started off with high hopes and good intentions. I hit the books hard at the beginning. However, studying was something I was not used to and I decided to find the easy way out. I found a place that sold CliffsNotes. The person who wrote the CliffsNotes must have been a C student because I had to cheat to get C's in the classes I attended, and just dropped out of the classes I was failing.

Needless to say, after the second semester my parents told me they would no longer pay my tuition or living expenses. They were not going to fund the college education of an average student. I moved back in with my parents, and they advised me to get a job. They offered me a job working for them in their antique store. I declined because the thought of working for my parents for the rest of my life frightened me. I pictured myself on Wall Street.

Then another image came to me: I saw myself flipping burgers for the rest of my life, and I shuddered at the thought. I knew I was meant to be a businessman, not an antique dealer or a burger flipper. However, I ended up flipping burgers until I got a job at Dimension Cable, under Fred Laraway. I became a door-to-door salesman, selling cable.

Meeting face to face with people from all walks of life, I learned how to interact with customers and be a salesman. I quickly became one of the highest producers there. I was making pretty good money for a nineteen-year-old.

My coworkers were older than me, from mid-twenties to early fifties, but I was making more money than they were. However, I couldn't see myself spending the rest of my life as a door-to-door salesman. I decided I wanted to go back to college.

The moment that shaped me more than anything occurred when I told my parents I was going back to ASU. They said "Good luck. We ain't paying for it!" I got into a huge argument with them. It was one of the worst fights I've ever had with my dad, and he kicked me out of the house. That day I called my buddies and asked them if they wanted to move out and get a place with me.

A week later I packed my stuff and moved out. As I was packing, my dad wrote me a five-page letter. He told me that I had gone through the first nineteen years of life being mediocre and accepting it. He said that I had put my friends and partying first. He explained that I was a bright kid, but I needed a plan and that I could do something special in my life if I had direction and motivation. Basically, he told me to get my head out of my ass. One of the most important things that he said in the letter is that he wanted to be proud of me.

As I type these words I have tears in my eyes, because to this day there is no bigger pleasure than seeing my parents proud of me. I have kept that letter over the years. It sits in the drawer of my nightstand, where I can pull it out and read it to remind myself that I don't have to accept mediocrity. Nothing has had more of an impact in my life than that five-page letter written by my father over twenty years ago. They were words that he wrote out of anger, desperation and frustration, but most of all out of love.

The Real Estate Detour

One day a buddy of mine and I were talking over a beer and he told me about his new job. He was a mortgage-loan officer, and was making a lot of money. He'd been in the business for almost a year, and his last paycheck was for $12,500. I didn't believe him, so he showed it to me. I remember saying to myself that if someone like him could make $12,500, then I sure could.

I was only bringing in about $500 a week. At that time, mortgage rates had begun to fall from double digits to single digits and borrowers everywhere were refinancing. There was a lot of money to be made. My friend was doing mailers, door knocking and talking to everyone he knew about the new rates.

I was used to going door to door. I was used to telling people about a product they could use. But I was making peanuts compared to him. Then it clicked in my head: he had a better product.

I applied for a loan officer's position where my buddy worked and waited for the business to roll in. I trained for a month to be a loan officer. But something happened the day I started. The refinance boom ended. Just like that. So did my high expectations. I was told that I was to change my focus to soliciting real estate agents for new loans.

I was about as green as could be. I was never sure I was using the right terminology. I didn't even really know what *escrow* meant. I mapped out a target area in a ten-mile radius from my office, and went from office to office talking to realtors. Some of them had been in the business for ages and they saw right through me.

I was spinning my wheels trying to make a connection with these realtors. I had never bought so many bagels and doughnuts in all my life. My buddy ended up moving to northern Arizona to open an office in Flagstaff, and I was making zero money as a loan officer.

My Real Estate Moment

It was abundantly clear to me that I was not a very good loan officer. I did meet a lot of realtors, but none of them wanted to use me as a loan officer. I had a credit card with a $1500 limit that I was using to schmooze the realtors and I was down to my last $150. I decided to take a couple of seasoned realtors, Bob and Mary Millard, out to breakfast. They had been in real estate since the '80s.

Bob and Mary liked my personality. They told me they didn't want to use me as a lender, but they thought I would make a great realtor. They told me I could be a realtor on the weekend and still go to school. (At that time, I was still enrolled at ASU.) They told me an average listing was about $150,000. I could make 3 percent off each sale and they would take 50 percent. I could sell one house a week. I did the math. That came out to $9,000 a month and I thought to myself, "Hell yes, I'm in!"

I was eager to find a direction, and real estate seemed to offer the opportunity to be successful. I decided to get my real estate license. I was pumped up and eager to get started.

Then I learned how much it cost to go to real estate school. Without much hope, I asked my parents for the money. To my surprise they said yes. I signed up for real estate school. Finally, I knew what I wanted to be.

I finished my classes and I passed my school test the first time. All I had to do now was pass the state test. The state test cost money. I didn't feel comfortable asking Bob and Mary for the money, even though I would promise to pay them back with my first commission. I thought my parents would say no. So I asked my girlfriend. She loaned me the money.

I knew I had only one shot to take this test and pass. I studied as hard as I could. I had never been so nervous in my life. I read the first question, and did not know the answer. The nerves set in and my hands were shaking. Nevertheless, I finished the test, and to my surprise I passed. I got my real estate license and joined the Millard Team.

The Millards had just listed a nice home in Chandler, Arizona, and they wanted me to do the open house. I had been in the business less than three days, but was eager to make some money. After all, I was about as broke as could be.

I began preparing for my first open house. I did all the right things. I placed ads in local newspapers and real estate magazines. I put open house signs all over the place. If you lived in the surrounding areas of my listing you knew I was having an open house. I used the last ten dollars on my credit card to buy doughnuts. I didn't even know if the sale would go through.

On Saturday it was show time. My open house officially started at 10:00 and was scheduled to be over by 2:00. I was there an hour early, preparing the home and placing the sign-in sheet prominently on a table near the front door.

With all my advertisements and sign placements I figured I probably should have brought along my girlfriend to help me meet and greet everyone who would show up.

The clock hit 10:00. Then 10:30. Then 10:50. Where were all the people? I nervously opened up one of the newspapers I had advertised in, to make sure I had the date, time and address correct. Sure enough, everything was right, but no one showed up at all. It was crazy. Then at about 1:30 a couple walked up to the house. I showed them around and they talked about what they were looking for in a home. I really got to know them, because, quite frankly, there was no one else to talk to.

They were the only two people who showed up that day. I held another open house on Sunday, and only got two people through that day as well. What a bust! Or so I thought . . .

On Monday morning I felt about as low as I could go. I was defeated and dejected. I dragged my feet all the way to the office, reluctant to tell my bosses about my failed open house. I walked into the office and told them the bad news: only four people had showed. "That's great!" they said. "You got four new leads. They all signed in, right? Do you have their contact information?"

Of course I had the sign-in sheet. I had their names and phone numbers. "Call them up and see if they're interested in seeing some homes." So I called all the leads on the sheet. Two of them set up appoints for the next day. I ended up selling two properties that day. I made $4,000 in one week. I realized at that moment that I could be successful in real estate. Just like that kid back in New York, I had figured out something that people wanted and that I could be the source to give it to them.

I knew I could build rapport with people. I was confident in my people skills. I could put a couple in my car and knew I could sell them a house. I wasn't really great at the paperwork, though. Mary helped me with that, and eventually I got an assistant to do that part of my job so I could focus on working my leads and selling houses.

Real estate is the type of career requiring you to be self-motivated to be successful. Many agents get their license and set up an office from home. I didn't want to be distracted at home, though. I was still going to college during that time. If I was not out showing houses or at school, I was in my office. I didn't want to miss a lead.

I worked for Bob and Mary at Realty Executives from 1994 to 1995. I quit the Millard team to be on my own when I felt confident I could handle all the aspects of my job. I stayed with Realty Executives, and became one of the top twenty-five agents in Arizona. I changed my major to real estate, and showed my father that I had heeded the advice he offered in his letter.

My Trust Deed Epiphany

The single greatest thing that happened to me in real estate happened quite by accident. Some might call that destiny. My parents had some good friends who lived in San Francisco, and they wanted to buy a place in Tempe. I knew they were looking on the high end, and I immediately gave them some options. I knew the market intimately and could find them not just the perfect home but also get the best price for them. This was back in 1999.

They flew down to Tempe, looked at some of the properties I had sent them and ultimately they bought one of the homes I had previewed for them at $1,150,000. My commission? $34,500. By far the single largest check I had ever received.

Needless to say, I was ecstatic. I was already a successful real estate agent, but now I was on another level. As a present to my parents, I bought them a top-of-the-line big-screen HDTV with part of my commission.

I was living in a nice house at the time, and frankly it was a bit more than I could afford, but it worked out all right. One thing that it didn't have was a wet bar. I wanted one just like one of my buddies had.

I called my friend and asked if I could come by and take some pictures of the bar he had built so I could show them to my contractor. He said, "Yeah, but I have to go to a trust deed sale first."

Immediately my ears perked up. A trust deed sale is simply a foreclosure where the lender auctions off the property to the highest bidder. I wanted to go along with him and just watch—trust deed sales were something I wanted to know more about, but frankly I was a bit intimidated.

I thought there would be perhaps a hundred investors all yelling and bidding, and scowling at the new guy. Me.

I couldn't have been more wrong. This particular sale took place at an attorney's office, and there were ten or twelve people around a conference table. The attorney went down the list of homes one by one, and I just watched.

Soon, a property address came up that was very familiar to me. It was a home in a neighborhood that I knew intimately and was easily worth $140,000. The successful bidder bought the home for $77,000.

I asked the winner of that home what he was going to do with it and he told me he was going to sell it. He told me that he would sell it to me right then and there for $10,000 more than what he paid for it: $87,000. It was still a remarkable deal.

I accepted his offer and asked for thirty days to get my financing lined up, but he told me that the deal was only good for twenty-four hours. I didn't have $80,000 but he gave me the number of a private lender for a hard-money loan.

The hard-money lender agreed to provide the loan with a 20 percent down payment, 18 percent interest and a $900 fee. I then thought, "You know, I'm going to wholesale this deal instead." (I'll explain wholesaling in more detail in Chapter 6.)

I immediately went back to my office and took out my Rolodex and began making calls. It was maybe the fourth or fifth number that I called when my client agreed to look at the property and buy it for $91,000. Eighty thousand dollars to the winning bidder at the auction and $4,000 for me. I also introduced him to the hard-money lender who arranged to provide the financing, and I closed my first wholesale transaction. I remember calling my dad and telling him my life had just changed. It was my "a-ha!" moment.

I had made $4,000 without using any of my own money, and it all happened in less than twenty-four hours. It hit me square in the face: I had found my calling. I had soon bought over three thousand houses from that very same attorney in the very same fashion. I was the wholesaling king, and everybody knew it.

You never, ever know when you're going to meet the person who will change your life forever.

CHAPTER 2
Where We Are Today

To clearly understand not just where we are today but what we might expect in the future we need to know how we got here. Today, most mortgage loans are underwritten to standards set out by the Federal Housing Administration (FHA), United States Department of Agriculture (USDA), Department of Veterans Affairs (VA), Federal National Mortgage Association (Fannie Mae) and the Federal Home Loan Corporation (Freddie Mac). These agencies issue approval guidelines for FHA, USDA, VA, Fannie Mae and Freddie Mac, respectively.

Over the years, mortgage lenders turned to these programs when borrowers sought financing. It's important to understand why these agencies exist in the first place. The primary reason is to facilitate homeownership. One of the ways homeownership is encouraged is by providing lenders with needed liquidity.

In the simplest example of how liquidity affects the real estate industry, imagine that a mortgage company has one million dollars in the bank and is in the business of making home loans. The lender then proceeds to make ten new home loans to their clients at $100,000 each. That's great, right? Sure it is, but guess what just happened? The mortgage company is out of money.

They can no longer issue mortgage loans, but must be satisfied with collecting interest each month. That's how mortgages used to be issued: by private banks who issued home loans financed by money in the bank's vault. The bank would approve the loan, and then collect the monthly interest while following its own internal approval guidelines. Banks still do that to some degree today, making loans using their own standards and keeping the loan in its own "portfolio."

However, today, to restore a mortgage lender's funds, once a loan is approved that loan may be sold in what is called the "secondary" market. A lender with one million dollars to lend can issue the mortgage approval, and then sell the loan to other mortgage companies or Fannie and Freddie, replenishing the coffers to continue making more loans.

The catch is that the loan must conform to specific guidelines laid out by each agency. There are minimum credit and income requirements for every loan today, and as long as the lender approves the loan under accepted standards and warrants that the loan meets those standards, the loan can be sold, providing needed liquidity.

Now let's review what happened in the early 2000s. A new breed of investors began issuing a different set of mortgage programs, with lower standards.

These subprime loans have always been around in one form or another. Subprime loans are so-called because the standards are lower than those that are below a loan labeled as prime. Subprime loans are primarily issued to borrowers with poor credit, and did in fact provide a needed service. In some cases they still do.

We all know that bad things can happen to good people, such as the loss of a job, an extended illness or some other catastrophic event that can wreak financial havoc on an individual's ability to repay a debt. Typically, though, the event is temporary and the individual has time to repair the credit and eventually get back on track.

Subprime loans allow for the path to repair by providing a home loan to those with poor credit. Once the borrower has repaid the subprime mortgage on time and repaired the credit profile, the borrower would then refinance out of the higher-priced subprime loan into a conventional one. The offset was higher rates and fees, as well as a hefty down payment.

Subprime loans in the early 2000s had down payment requirements of at least 25 percent, and for those with a recent bankruptcy a 50 percent down payment wasn't uncommon. Subprime lenders typically kept their loans in-house, as there wasn't a secondary market hungry to purchase such loans.

But a secondary market soon formed and investors were hungry for the loans. Mortgage loans are considered some of the most secure, as borrowers will do whatever they can to keep their home. If the homeowners do in fact lose their home to foreclosure, the home could be sold to recover the loan amount.

Another niche in the mortgage industry began to form: loans deemed "alternative." Alternative lending simply meant the loans were an alternative to Fannie, Freddie, VA, FHA and

USDA fare. Such loans had their own guidelines as well, but were famous for not verifying critical aspects of the loan file.

These loans didn't verify employment or income, and the lender used the information on the loan application without verification. Such mortgage programs were called "stated" loans, because whatever the borrower stated, the lender used. Other loans, called "no document" loans, crept into the marketplace. For these, nothing at all was on the credit report except the identity of the borrower.

One of the primary reasons homeownership hit record levels was the fact that just about anyone could qualify for a home loan. Alternative and subprime lenders focused on a market share that traditional lenders didn't touch. Soon, these lenders expanded their market share to the point that traditional lenders were rapidly losing their own share of the housing pie.

As each new market was formed and saturated, alternative lenders introduced yet another program that expanded the loan program to include still more potential buyers. Someone with a 450 credit score could get a mortgage with a 20 percent down payment but had to verify income with tax returns.

Once that market was established, the lender would then reduce the down payment requirement to include still more potential borrowers. Soon income wasn't being verified, and then verification of assets also disappeared. Down payments were reduced and guidelines were relaxed to reach more and more borrowers. And investors still bought these mortgage loans with an apparently insatiable appetite.

The reason this worked in the past was because of the notion that real estate in the United States would always increase in value and if something bad happened and the owner couldn't pay the mortgage, the investors were safe because the home could always be sold to yet another buyer to pay off the previous mortgage.

Traditional lenders took notice and began to tread the path of subprime and alternative lenders by offering similar programs to try to recover lost market share.

Fannie and Freddie both relaxed their underwriting guidelines, allowing for a loan approval with lower credit standards. There were loan programs that didn't verify income that in the past would never make it past the application process when applying for a conventional loan.

You can now understand why home appreciation rates hit record levels in many areas of the country, with buyers bidding against one another for real estate, hoping to cash in on the rapid rise in prices. New developments were sold out as quickly as they could be built and the real estate market was on a roll.

Then the music stopped.

At some point, there were no more buyers to sell to. The market was saturated. And investors who bought houses with the intent of flipping them and selling for a profit found out that no one wanted to buy any longer.

Borrowers who couldn't afford the monthly payments were the first of the dominos to fall. Homeowners wanting or needing to sell found they weren't able to, so they reduced their asking prices. Values began to fall below what borrowers owed on their homes, meaning homes couldn't sell without the owner coming to the closing table with thousands of dollars.

The subprime and alternative mortgage programs that originally provided a valued service to the real estate industry by allowing individuals to get back on their feet and start a new future found out that the loans they took were more toxic than ever. Both loan types primarily featured so-called "hybrid" loans.

A hybrid mortgage is in fact an adjustable-rate loan, but is fixed for a predetermined period of time, say three or five years. This initial fixed period keeps the payment stable for the borrowers, while providing a period during which the borrowers can repair their credit.

However, at the end of the initial fixed term, the loan would adjust, but differently from conventional adjustable-rate-mortgage loans found at any mortgage lender today.

These hybrid loans would adjust to a level that might be three or four times higher than what the borrowers were originally qualified for. Put yourself in that situation and ask what would happen if your mortgage payment quadrupled.

Borrowers' mortgage payments quickly rose to unaffordable levels and they couldn't sell their homes due to the collapse in the real estate market.

Values continued to plunge and foreclosures hit record levels. Banks closed their doors and investment firms with addresses on Wall Street failed. Fannie Mae and Freddie Mac were taken over by the federal government.

Billions of taxpayer dollars were thrown at Fannie, Freddie and FHA to keep them solvent. Economies here and abroad were sideswiped and the United States entered what is now known as the Great Recession.

There were more foreclosures than ever before and no region was left untouched at some level. This new landscape offered an unprecedented opportunity for real estate investors. People just like you and me.

The New Landscape

Alternative and subprime lenders vanished. The loans that put Fannie, Freddie and FHA near collapse were no longer issued. By the way, if you're wondering at this point about VA and USDA loans—they never changed their standards, and in fact VA loans historically have the lowest delinquency rates of any mortgage program in the marketplace, in spite of the fact that the loans require no money down.

The boomerang took full effect and mortgage lenders pulled back on their loan approvals. Lenders became almost paranoid to issue a mortgage loan, fearful that the economic crisis was far from over. But eventually the economy recovered, albeit slowly, and home prices began to stabilize.

The new landscape means all mortgage loans today must have all the information in the file verified. In a sense, lending has returned to its traditional, logical roots before the "Roaring 2000s." So what exactly is the new landscape?

Lenders will ask if you have a down payment and can prove your income and have good credit. We'll discuss financing options in more detail in Chapter 7, but you should know that the days of "stated" and "no documentation" loans are long gone. In fact, the Consumer Financial Protection Bureau (CFPB) now requires lenders to validate the Ability to Repay (ATR) for the borrower. Lenders do this by reviewing a debt-to-income ratio. The debt-to-income ratio is expressed as a percentage, and the ATR rule stipulates that the ratio be no greater than 43 percent.

If a borrower makes $10,000 per month, monthly debt—including debt from the new mortgage—may not exceed $4,300 using this example. We'll show you how to offset all of the mortgage payment with rental income from the property in Chapter 7.

The CFPB also laid groundwork for what is called a qualified mortgage, or QM. As long as a lender implements the guidelines of a QM loan, the lender receives certain legal protections from borrower and class-action lawsuits as a result of a loan approval. These new guidelines eliminate the "interest only" loan that was popular with the alternative-lending crowd.

Loans that had a negative amortization feature are not QM eligible. Negative amortization on a loan means a loan balance can actually increase if the borrower makes an optional lower loan payment each month. There are no balloon mortgages in the QM program, and closing costs may not exceed 3 percent of the amount borrowed. These rules are in addition to the CFPB-required ATR statute.

Lending stability has allowed housing prices to gradually rise since early 2012. Real estate investors have been snapping up these properties at record rates, and there has been no better time to invest in real estate than now. How can I make such a claim?

The first reason is inventory. A record number of foreclosures mean a record number of opportunities. There have always been foreclosures and real estate investors can be successful in almost any market at any time, regardless of the economic circumstances. Today there are simply so many homes waiting to be purchased at below-market values. Second, price stabilization means properties will continue to appreciate, providing additional equity. And finally, interest rates are still near record levels. This will change as mortgage rates can change even on a daily basis, but a gradual recovery keeps mortgage rates at manageable levels.

No, mortgage rates won't dip toward 2 percent, but they also won't get near 7 percent like we saw in 2007, and certainly not the 8 percent seen in the early part of the last decade.

When you combine low rates with low housing prices, the opportunity for real estate investors is better than anything we've experience in our lifetimes. What will the future look like?

To look forward, we have to examine the past. And what did we find out? We found out that too many speculators hit the market with no way of paying back the mortgage. We found out that easy money means easy disaster. We found out that mortgage lenders who prey on the unprepared are no longer around and will never return.

CHAPTER 3
The Foreclosure Process

Something went wrong. Very wrong. When a home goes into foreclosure, something happens that changes the entire financial landscape of the borrower. Lenders don't like to foreclose. In fact, they loathe it. Contrary to what some may think, lenders don't like to make a mortgage loan for the sole purpose of foreclosing on it later. If they did, they wouldn't be lenders very long; they would be closed-up shops.

When a mortgage lender accepts a loan application from a prospective borrower, the lender evaluates three basic characteristics of the borrower. The lender looks at the credit history of the applicant and determines whether or not the applicant has provided evidence of a responsible payment history to other creditors.

The lender also looks at the income of the applicant to make sure the potential borrower makes enough money each month to pay for the new mortgage, property taxes, insurance and other current monthly obligations. The mortgage company will also verify that the borrower has enough money in the bank to be used for a down payment plus closing costs associated with a potential transaction.

Finally, the lender reviews the physical asset—the collateral. The property being financed. The lender will make sure the value of the property is what the sales contract says it is by ordering a property appraisal and that the home is in good condition.

But very little of that occurred over the past ten years. The lenders that didn't pay attention to credit or income are out of the business altogether. In fact, today there are laws that require a lender to prove the potential borrower has the ability to repay the mortgage should the loan be approved.

There are no more "stated" loans, in which the borrower doesn't have to document income, employment or money in the bank. And while there are still a few subprime lenders around, the loan is completely documented and down payment amounts of 30 percent or more are required.

Yet, when a foreclosure notice is filed, the borrower's world is turned upside down. And believe it or not, the lender wants to help the owner as much as possible. Why would a lender want to keep a home from being foreclosed upon when the lender can simply take back the home with a foreclosure?

If a lender is forced to foreclose on the property and take back the collateral, the lender automatically loses money. There is no more interest being paid on the note and there are probably back property taxes that must be paid. Legal fees mount and other services that must be accounted for accrue.

When a lender has too many foreclosures, the cost of the lender's funds is increased. That makes the lender's interest rates too high compared to other mortgage companies and the lender will soon go out of business.

Lenders want to have the highest-performing loans as possible, and zero foreclosures. That will provide the lender with a steady source of funds to make still more loans and offer some of the most competitive rates in the market.

But when the borrower misses payments, a foreclosure may be the only tool the lender has. A borrower doesn't want to go into foreclosure. There is nothing more damaging to a borrower's credit score than a foreclosure. It's the ultimate default. Even a bankruptcy can't top the damage a foreclosure can cause. But it can be unavoidable and is the last course of action a lender will take.

Why did the borrower suddenly have problems making the mortgage payment? The prime candidate is a sudden loss of income. As the economy spiraled downward during the Great Recession, millions lost their jobs. And of course without a job there's little income.

There can be unemployment compensation for the newly unemployed, but not everyone qualifies for unemployment benefits and for those that do the income is hardly enough to cover living expenses the homeowner is used to.

There can also be a situation of a divorce. When two people apply for a mortgage together and both incomes are needed to qualify, a divorce changes the financial structure.

Sometimes the person who gets to keep the house finds out the reduced monthly income isn't enough to cover the mortgage payment. If the homeowner can't make the monthly payments, a foreclosure may be on the way.

Worse than a loss of job or a divorce is an extended illness or even a death in the family, which can create a situation where recovery is impossible. In any scenario, a foreclosure is sparked by a series of unfortunate events. Savings can be depleted and credit severely damaged, but without the foreclosure process the mortgage industry could not survive.

Lenders would not make any mortgage loan without the assurance of being able to take back the asset if the owners didn't live up to the original loan agreement, regardless of the cause. Lenders don't want to foreclose. They want the owner to begin making payments again.

The basic foreclosure process works basically the same way across the country, with few variances. Mortgage payments are typically due on the first of the month, and if not made on or before the fifteenth, a late penalty is assessed. A common late penalty is 5 percent of the payment.

When a borrower misses payment on the first of the month, the lender hardly notices. There's a grace period, after all. If the fifteenth comes and goes, a late penalty is applied and the lender waits for the payment. As the end of the month approaches, the lender will begin a series of initial collection efforts with phone calls and a letter, wondering why the borrower has missed the payment due earlier this month.

When the borrower misses the subsequent payment due on the first, the mortgage lender gets a little more nervous. Missing two payments in a row means the lender will issue a formal notice called a Notice of Default, sometimes referred to as an NOD.

The NOD is mailed by certified letter to the property owners' mailing address. The NOD is also a public record and the notice is filed in the county records. The NOD contains the owner's name and the property address of the delinquent home.

The NOD also clearly spells out that the loan is in default and has an amount the borrower needs to give to the lender, in certified funds, that will bring the loan current and a warning that if the loan is not brought current then a foreclosure filing will occur and the owner could forfeit the property. Again, this notice is filed in the public record for anyone to see. At least anyone who wants to see a list of homes that are dangerously close to a foreclosure.

At this stage, the lender may not file a foreclosure notice until the next payment is missed, as noted in the NOD. It is in this period that the owner can make just one payment instead of the two that are due and can forestall the foreclosure filing. This can only happen when three payments in a row are missed, so if the owner makes a payment before the third is missed, the foreclosure cannot be filed.

During this time, the owner can work with the lender for a loan modification. A loan modification is a procedure that changes certain parts of the note but does not replace the note.

A loan modification's most common use is to reduce the interest rate on the mortgage to better accommodate the owner's current financial situation. For example, the owner has a 6 percent fifteen-year mortgage loan, but may be able to afford an interest rate of 2 percent and a thirty-year term.

When a property owner applies for a loan modification, most lenders will hold off on filing for a foreclosure; however, many go ahead and make the filing if the third payment is missed but hold off on the foreclosure unless needed.

The borrower will complete a loan modification application that the lender will use to determine if a loan modification can help. If the household had two incomes on the original loan application but now only has one, the lender may elect to modify the note that will allow the owners to continue making the mortgage payment at the reduced level.

However, there's still the possibility that the lender can't modify the interest rate so it is low enough to make the payments affordable. Or it could be a situation where there is no income at all. If the lender can't make a loan modification work, the foreclosure process will continue.

If the third payment is indeed missed, the foreclosure filing is made and the lender takes the steps necessary to take back the home. The foreclosure filing, like the NOD, is also a public record. It's important to note here that just because a foreclosure notice is filed it doesn't mean the foreclosure is in fact imminent. Sometimes the filing is there for the protection of the lender.

For example, the owners may be able to work out an arrangement where the past-due payments are paid out over time, included with the existing mortgage payment.

Sometimes during a financial emergency, when the mortgage payment can't be made, it's a challenge to come up with two or even three payments. Say someone lost their job and missed three payments but found new work. While the entire past-due amount can't be paid, the owner can pay out the past-due amounts in installments.

In some instances, once the borrowers get back on their feet, the lender can agree to put the past-due balances on the end of the note, relieving the requirement to make up the past-due balances. Lenders can perform a variety of actions that can help to avoid a foreclosure, and as long as the borrowers are communicating with the lender, the foreclosure can be stalled and ultimately avoided.

But when there is no communication, the lender feels there is no other choice. Why would someone not work out a deal with the lender, or even return a phone call?

It may not make any sense at all when someone doesn't respond to a lender's repeated requests to contact them. Why lose the property unnecessarily? Take a minute, however, and put yourself in the shoes of someone who is experiencing a financial change they would have never imagined.

Just as a lender doesn't issue a mortgage approval with the intention of foreclosing on the property, a borrower doesn't complete a mortgage application with the intention of having the property taken away due to nonpayment. That makes less sense than not returning collection calls, right?

Someone may be enjoying life and the day-to-day activities that go along with it when suddenly their employer lets them go, there is a divorce or extended illness. Whatever the circumstance, it's bad. And when something like that happens, there are few places for someone in that situation to turn.

You can go next door to chat with your neighbor about last night's game, but who goes to their neighbor and says, "I just got laid off, I don't think I'll be able to pay my bills and my house is being foreclosed upon"? It just doesn't happen that way. Most homeowners feel too embarrassed.

A homeowner misses two payments in a row and then certified letters and repeated telephone calls begin and the owner doesn't know what to do. There's nowhere to turn, and perhaps the only thing the owner can do is ignore the entire situation, frozen in fear.

The owner may feel that talking to the lender is useless: he or she can't pay the past due amounts anyway, so why even bother? The owner is not only afraid but confused, with nowhere to turn.

Yes, there are those who have little problem in walking away from a property and handing over the keys, but they are rare. A homeowner can take years to build a solid credit profile, and then within just a few short months all that is wiped away due to circumstances beyond the borrower's control.

Depending upon where the property is located, the foreclosure can be a judicial or a non-judicial one. Each state has its own guidelines on which method a lender must follow. A judicial foreclosure means the foreclosure must be heard in front of a judge. The lender sues the borrowers and they are provided with a notice to appear in court. The lender then proves their case, and the borrowers can plead theirs. However, the case is most often simply that the borrower can no longer make payments and that the original mortgage document validates that the lender has the right to foreclose. Depending upon the court's case load, appeals and other factors, it can take more than a year for a foreclosure to finally take place.

Non-judicial states require no such court appearance, and as long as the lender filed the proper paperwork the home can be foreclosed upon much more quickly. In as little as forty-five days (in some states) the home is sold on the courthouse steps to the highest bidder.

When a lender sends a property to the county to complete the foreclosure process with an auction, the lender will typically have a minimum amount it will accept. If the lender requires the successful bid be no lower than $75,000 and the bids are no higher than $50,000, then the home goes back into the lender's inventory in an area called the Real Estate Owned (REO) department.

That's the foreclosure process, and there are lender protections as well as borrower protections inserted in the original loan documents. Many who have financed real estate in the past will remember that there is specific language, often in bold print, that explains when the payments are due, when a late fee can be assessed and what happens if they fail to make the mortgage payments.

It's often the case that borrowers who are excited to close on their purchase skim over the multitude of paperwork in the loan file and don't pay any attention to the clause, but that clause is there to provide the lender with its legal recourse.

At the same time, individual states have their own consumer protection laws prohibiting a lender from taking back a home unless a specific procedure is followed. These rules are strict and cannot be waived. You may recall the lawsuits that were filed over the previous few years by attorneys representing clients in foreclosure.

One of these suits addressed "robo signing" of foreclosure documents. Foreclosure filings are required to be individually reviewed and signed by the person making the review. Due to the unprecedented number of foreclosure filings, many lenders, to save time, hired individuals who did nothing more than sign foreclosure papers with no review at all.

Lenders who were guilty of this practice paid millions of dollars in fines and had a large number of foreclosure filings deemed void because the correct procedure was not followed. That didn't necessarily cancel a foreclosure; it just postponed one until the proper procedures were followed.

Once the foreclosure has been completed, there is still the notion of the unpaid mortgage. Is the owner who has already lost the home due to foreclosure still obligated to pay the mortgage back?

A foreclosure moves the asset from the borrower back to the bank, but depending upon state law after the foreclosure, the bank may still pursue additional legal action, forcing the former owner to continue to pay the past-due mortgage.

Say that the lender foreclosed on a home with an outstanding mortgage balance of $100,000 but the auction only brought in $75,000. The lender may then seek a deficiency judgment by going to court yet again and attempting to recover the $25,000 deficit. Various states have different rules regarding deficiency judgment procedures but it's possible to still be entangled with the lender after the foreclosure and the auction have taken place.

CHAPTER 4
Foreclosure Sources

Now that we know how the foreclosure process works, when and where do we find these below-market bargains? Excellent question! In fact, as with anything new, there will be lots of queries because you are still exploring a brand-new world. And that's why you're reading this book: to gain knowledge from me that will secure your financial future for you and your heirs. How many foreclosures are we talking about?

In 2008, there were almost three million foreclosures filed across the country, with certain areas bearing the brunt. Arizona, California and Nevada took some of the worst of it. Since then? According to RealtyTrac, a leading real estate data firm, the numbers are as follows:

2009	3.5 million
2010	3.8 million
2011	3.9 million
2012	2.3 million
2013	1.4 million

As you can see, foreclosure filings hit a peak in 2011 but have fallen off since then. Does that seem like foreclosures should be falling from the trees? After all, 2013 was only about one-third of the 2011 count. Are there any left? Of course there are. Plenty.

It's just that when looking at such staggering numbers, the 1.4 million seems a bit paltry, doesn't it? But that's still a considerable amount of volume. Compare that with 2000's volume of 470,000, or 640,000 in 2004.

Yes, investors were still buying and selling foreclosures then as they are today. Foreclosures will always be a solid method to build wealth. But you still need to go find them. Where do you start?

Remember the Process?

Homeowners don't put a sign in their yard that says something like, "Hey, I'm having trouble making my mortgage payments and I'll soon go into foreclosure. Someone feel free to call me and buy my house. Fast."

That would be convenient, but then there would be hundreds if not thousands of offers, and the price might be driven up to the point that it's no longer a bargain. No, homeowners don't advertise that they're having financial problems. The neighbors usually don't know. Maybe close family members do. But in reality, anyone can find out if they know where to look. It's in the public record, as we explained in the previous chapter.

Recall that lenders are required to provide offic
borrowers who fall behind on their payments and
primary steps before foreclosing on the property.

The first is the Notice of Default, mailed via certified letter
when the borrower misses two payments in a row. Note that a
borrower can miss every other payment and sometimes nothing
will happen, other than that their credit report at this stage is
pretty much shot. But when two in a row are missed, the legal
wheels begin to turn.

The NOD is filed at the county recorder's office as a matter
of public record, as well as published in a local newspaper. In
some states, different statutes may apply regarding when and
where the NOD is filed, but most pre-foreclosure notices start
with the NOD once two payments in a row go missing.

If the next payment is missed, then a foreclosure filing will
also be sent via certified mail, this time possibly by an attorney
representing the lender, or directly from the lender itself. This
too is a public record and also published in a local newspaper.

The first place to look for foreclosure filings is at the county
recorder's office, as well as to review the section in the newspaper that publishes certain public records.

You can do this on your own, and many who start investing
in foreclosures start out in this way, by a physical visit to the local county recorder. The foreclosure filing will list the property
address, the owner, the amount due, the mortgage company and
any additional information.

What you're concerned with at this point is contacting the
owner directly before the foreclosure auction actually takes

place. What else can you find in a filing? All sorts of information. You can find out how big the home is, what the county assessed the property for, if it's residential or commercial and the value of the land, as well as improvements made. Certain states provide more information than others, but most provide this information at minimum.

Let's say a property owner falls behind and a foreclosure notice is filed. Because it's a public record, the homeowner might soon see a letter or two in the mailbox from people he's never met offering to buy the house and avoid foreclosure. "How do they know about this?" the homeowner may ask, not realizing that two public filings have been made with the owner's name on it.

Remember, the owner is afraid and confused and may feel as if there is nowhere to turn. The owner doesn't have enough money to bring the loan current and really doesn't see any way out of his situation. But you can provide a way out. And by presenting yourself as someone who can help them avoid a foreclosure altogether and keep that off of the credit report, you're a savior.

Sometimes eager "helpers" approach the owner in the worst possible way by saying something to the effect of, "Hey, I found out you're in foreclosure because it's in the public record and anyone can find that out. Sell me your house before you lose everything." That's too harsh and doesn't take into consideration the owner's emotions at the time.

Instead, try something like, "I work with homeowners just like you, and I'm sorry that you're going through all this. It happens to so many people these days, but if you'd like to talk about selling the property quickly to avoid any future action, I'm here to help. I'll give you a fair price and can close within just a few days. If you'd like, I can write a formal letter for your lender to include along with a sales contract. That way you don't lose all your equity in your home and the foreclosure won't happen."

This is a softer, more empathetic approach. Don't expect a ton of responses if you do nothing more than send out pre-printed postcards to those whose names appear in the public record. Instead, compose a handwritten letter and handwrite the address on the front of the envelope. Avoid anything that looks like a mass mailing. Personalization and empathy work best when dealing directly with the property owner.

Once you have a contract signed, the lender will typically halt foreclosure proceedings, allowing you time to close the deal. With your signed contract, make sure you include a preapproval letter from your lender or proof of funds if you will be paying in cash. You want to convince the lender you're serious and have the means to carry through with the purchase.

Searching foreclosure filings and buying the property before the auction takes place is the most common, proven technique. But there will be competitors who will also contact the owner, offering various proposals. One way to cut down on the competition is to contact the owner before the foreclosure notice is filed. It is optimal to contact the owner right after the NOD and before the foreclosure filing.

When the initial notice is filed, typically the owner needs to just make one more payment to keep the delinquencies past due for one payment, not two. By making one mortgage payment before the third one is missed, the process can start all over again. It's not uncommon for multiple notices to be sent to an owner who falls behind on two payments but consistently makes a payment before a third payment in a row is missed, triggering the foreclosure notice. This means you may be contacting an owner with less likelihood of success, because the owner staves off the foreclosure.

However, by contacting the owner with a handwritten letter or even visiting the property yourself, you'll be first in line to get to the owner. At some point, the owner may simply throw up his hands and call you and say, "Let's talk, I'm tired of all this."

But it all starts with a visit to the county recorder's office. Some investors hire individuals to visit the office every thirty days or so for an update without your having to visit the county recorder on your own.

Foreclosure Services

You may also take advantage of companies that do the research on their own and publish foreclosure information taken from local county records, banks or other sources. Instead of visiting a government office for a list of foreclosures, you can log on to the internet and visit websites that are dedicated to providing lists of foreclosed properties, for a fee.

You can decide which state, city or county you'd like to research and you will receive a regular list of homes that have been foreclosed upon or are in the bank's possession. These sites are easy to research, but recognize that anyone with an internet connection can subscribe to the very same service, so there may be considerable competition. More competitors drive up the price.

Auctions

Remember that different states will have slightly different rules regarding foreclosures and filings, but there are a number of common procedures.

One place where you will find foreclosures is at an auction. The auction typically takes place on the courthouse steps or in an office with other bidders. A listing of the various properties is placed in the public record and posted for all interested parties to see.

The lender who forecloses on the property will usually provide a minimum bid. The bid is a combination of the mortgage on the property, interest due and other charges the lender would like to recover. The lender has the ability to make the initial bid, but after that bid is made or the lender declines, the other bidders can start the auction process.

The winning bidder then must pay either in cash or a cashier's check, and depending upon the rules of the area the bidder may have twenty-four hours to pay or the payment is due when the gavel falls for the winning bid. The rules are easy to find simply by contacting the county and asking for the guidelines that auctioneers must follow and other details.

REO

What happens if the lender doesn't get the minimum bid needed? Then the property goes back to the bank. To a place the bank really wishes it didn't have—the REO department. REO stands for Real Estate Owned, and is the lender's division that keeps and manages properties that have been foreclosed upon and not yet sold. This is where you can find foreclosed properties for sale.

Big banks will have lots of foreclosed homes in their REO departments. These lenders have their own websites listing their foreclosed properties for sale in every state in the Union. Instead of calling a bank and asking for its REO department, you can instead log on to the bank's site dedicated to REOs. Such lenders typically have agreements with local real estate brokers who help manage, list and show the foreclosed properties to potential buyers.

Such properties have typically been maintained, and repaired when needed, and any title issues have usually been resolved. If you simply drive through a neighborhood and see an agent's "For Sale" sign with a rider underneath that says "Foreclosure," the agent has a listing agreement with the lender to market the property.

You may have better results with a bank's REO department when you work with a local or regional bank that does not have a national presence. Smaller banks that survived the housing crisis still have real estate on their books they'd rather not have. They're a non-performing asset, and harm their credit profile and increase their reserve requirements. Too many foreclosed properties on the books can shut a bank down completely.

Here is where the personal touch comes into play again. Contact the REO manager and schedule a meeting. Better yet, take the manager to lunch. Treat it as a sales call and let the bank know that you're a real estate investor and have access to capital that allows you to close within days when needed.

Too many would-be investors simply leave a voice mail with a bank's REO department and never establish a working relationship with the REO division. If you're able to show the bank that you're a serious player and you can do what you say you can do, it's possible you'll be alerted to a new addition to the bank's REO department before anyone else. Don't take shortcuts to this approach with emails or postcards. Establish a true, working relationship.

Probate

What happens when someone becomes an "instant" landlord and inherits a property from a passing family member? To the person who just inherited the home it's a brand-new experience. And it can be a hassle, especially if the home is located far away in another state. Estates are handled with a probate attorney who makes sure that the personal property and obligations of the deceased property owner are handled according to state law.

Many times, the new owners have no desire to own the real estate or rent it out, and would rather just sell the property. Just as making a personal visit to a bank's REO department yields rewards, so too does making yourself known to the probate attorneys in your area.

When the heirs of a property ask the attorney, "How can we sell this property?" you want to be at the forefront. Make sure you're a known fixture in the probate business and distribute your contact information before an opportunity presents itself.

Family Law

A probate attorney will often also specialize in family law. Such a discipline takes care of legal matters that involve family, such as adoption, wills or a divorce. When a couple files for a divorce, they may need someone who can buy their home quickly.

When there is real property involved in a divorce proceeding and the final divorce decree awards the home to one party and perhaps the mortgage payments to another, the mortgage company isn't all that concerned about what the judge said in the ruling. Just because the judge said that one party is no longer responsible for the mortgage payment, the lender doesn't necessarily have to agree. The loan documents originally signed by both the husband and wife don't have a clause that says something to the effect of: "If you get divorced, we'll agree to whatever the court says." Not at all. The lender approved the loan with both parties on the note, regardless of what the judge says.

For example, say a couple gets a divorce and the husband keeps the house and the wife moves on. The husband has agreed to pay the mortgage. But sometimes he's late. Later, the ex-wife applies for a new loan, only to discover that there are multiple late payments on her credit report. Late payments on a mortgage are the worst kind when a lender evaluates a mortgage application.

The new lender may consider the divorce decree but is not forced to. The only way for the wife to get off of the mortgage as well as the title is if the husband applies for a refinance on his own, removing the ex-wife from the original loan as well as title.

But what if the husband has trouble refinancing? He will if he's been late on his mortgage payment. Perhaps the couple needed both payments to qualify for the original loan, and now the husband who lives in the home has trouble every month paying the mortgage on time. At some stage, it's possible that home will go into foreclosure and both the husband and wife will have their credit damaged.

To avoid negative credit and a possible foreclosure, you can step in and buy the property from the owners, relieving both from the obligation and transferring the property to you. By making regular contact with local family lawyers who specialize in divorce, you can come up with potential leads. You won't find as many potential deals compared to a bank's REO department, but at the same time you will have little, if any, competition. By moving quickly to purchase a home from a distressed couple, you're ensuring their credit won't be damaged and they can move on with their private lives.

Bandit Signs

What's a bandit sign? You may not have heard the term before, but you've likely seen them at an intersection or along the roadway. They are one of the most cost-effective means to find home-owners who are facing possible foreclosure.

A bandit sign is a handwritten sign that appears at the base of a stop sign or stapled on a utility pole that says something to the effect of "We pay cash for your home!" or "Stop Foreclosure! Cash Buyer!" or some other call to action. The signs themselves are almost universal in construction and composed of "Coroplast," which is a corrugated, weather-resistant material. Political campaign signs use the same material. Why are they called bandit signs? That's the nickname given to them because they often don't stay where they're initially placed for very long. Someone decides they don't like the sign and pulls it out of the ground. A local ordinance may prohibit such signage and they're removed. If you're not sure if a bandit sign is legal where you want to place them, a simple phone call to the city can answer your question.

Bandit signs are cheap. In fact, the most expensive part of the sign isn't the sign but the metal stand, and any sign company can provide you with both the signs and the stands. The more resourceful know to contact local politicians just after an election.

Most areas require that campaigns remove their signs within a certain period after an election and these campaign offices may have hundreds of signs they have no idea what to do with. Call them and offer to take the metal stands from them for free!

Don't have the printer preprint your message for you. Bandit signs are more effective when they're handwritten with a magic marker on a plain white background and placed at an intersection where drivers must stop their cars or alongside on and off ramps from roads and highways. Just like any other advertising message, those who need to sell their property fast will pay attention and those who don't won't.

The message must be clear and to the point, and must provide your phone number. How can you close in days? We'll discuss that in more detail in the next chapter. The short version is that either you can pay cash out of your bank account, or, if have a private or hard-money lender at your disposal, you can close in a matter of days, compared to weeks that a traditional mortgage approval may require.

Bird Dogs

A "bird dog" is the industry term for a person who does a lot of the legwork for you. Depending upon the degree of work performed, the bird dog may provide you with nothing more than a list of addresses for you to look at or provide a complete analysis on a potential purchase.

Bird dogs get paid by finding deals instead of buying them as their own investments. In fact, many real estate investors either get started as a bird dog or supplement their investment activity by passing along potential deals to other investors.

Bird dogs find potential deals just as any other investor might, but some investors prefer to concentrate on other areas of the business. For example, a bird dog is might be driving through a neighborhood, as he often does, to see if there are any changes or new "For Sale" signs in the area. He notices that a recent "For Sale By Owner" sign is gone, so he stops and walks up to the house and asks the owner if the property was sold and, if he doesn't mind, what it finally sold for.

The owner tells him that he didn't sell the property because he wanted to regroup. The bird dog tells him that he knows of someone who could pay cash for his house. Would he sell if the price were right? "Sure," the owner replies, and the bird dog begins preparing the information needed to present to his various investors.

Good bird dogs have multiple investors in their database. Once the right investor decides to purchase the property, the bird dog steps aside and lets the transaction take place. The bird dog will get paid based upon a percentage of the profit when the home is flipped, on a per-transaction basis or a combination of both. It's up to the bird dog and the investor.

Networking

This is a constant. You must always be networking, whether it's between just you and a colleague or at a luncheon with others. Everyone you meet must know that you're a real estate investor and are always in the market for the right deal. By getting out and meeting as many people as you can, soon you'll begin to get referrals. What are some of the ways you can get your name out?

Networking clubs abound in most cities in some capacity. These clubs are business referral organizations that meet regularly, have lunch or drinks together and share information about what each person does and what they're looking for.

Many meetings allow a few people five minutes or so to stand up and present their wants and needs to the rest of the members. These networking clubs can be open to any sort of business, from a plumber to an accountant, but they all have the same purpose, which is to get more business. If you refer someone to a plumber in the group you expect the plumber to reciprocate.

Other clubs specialize in a particular industry. Cities across the country have real estate investment clubs. Here, like-minded individuals meet regularly to catch up on local real estate trends, hear presentations by industry professionals and exchange information. Whether you're new or a veteran real estate investor, joining and attending a real estate investment club will shorten the learning curve greatly.

You'll find real estate agents, bankers, private lenders, insurance agents, property inspectors, contractors and anyone else even remotely related to the real estate industry. At the very minimum, you'll learn things from the pros without having to pick up that information the hard way, and you'll have fun doing it.

CHAPTER 5
The Foreclosure Purchase

So far we've discovered how we got where we are today, the foreclosure process and the steps that lenders must take, as well as where to look for foreclosures and other properties that are near that stage. Okay, but what happens when you find an ideal property you'd like to buy? How do you buy that foreclosure?

It's much like any other real estate purchase, but you've really got some homework to do before you decide on going to any closing at all. There's a bit of due diligence necessary to make sure you're buying what you think you're buying.

And depending upon where you find the property and who is selling, your process must adapt. Let's start with what is perhaps the basic purchase, in which you buy a property directly from the property owner before the home goes into foreclosure.

From the Owner

We all know that real estate isn't your typical everyday purchase. No, you'll need resources beyond your checking account, and that means finding reliable sources of financing. There are three basic types: conventional, private and an investor pool.

Conventional loans are those underwritten and approved using conventional guidelines issued by Fannie Mae and Freddie Mac. They are by far the most competitive long-term financing programs available. This is primarily because there are more Fannie and Freddie loans issued (both for owner-occupied as well as investor properties) than any other loan programs in the market today.

When there is more of anything, the price tends to be more competitive. These loans are no different and should be your first choice when buying a property with the intention of keeping it for the long term.

A conventional mortgage will have an interest rate a bit higher than a loan for a primary residence, with a common spread being about one-quarter to one-half percent. If you can get a thirty-year conventional mortgage for an owner-occupied home at 4.5 percent, an investor loan would be in the 4.75 to 5 percent range. How are conventional mortgages approved and what can you expect?

You'll need at minimum a down payment of 20 percent of the sales price. For a $100,000 home, that's $20,000. If you have 25 percent down, your interest rate will be lower by about .125 percent or so. There's no getting around the down payment amount, so expect to pay at least 20 percent from your own funds.

The lender will verify these funds are yours by examining your bank statements over the previous two to three months. Funds for down payment and closing costs can't be borrowed or otherwise unsecured; they must be at your disposal and belong to you with your name on the account.

Your credit will be evaluated, and today lenders use credit scores—commonly referred to as FICO scores, named after the company that developed the credit algorithm, Fair Isaac Corporation.

It should be noted here that credit scores for mortgages are calculated differently than scores for automobile loans or other credit lines. While scores from these other uses may be similar, they typically won't be the same.

A credit score is a three-digit number reflecting the likelihood of default. The scores range from 300 to 850, with the higher scores representing better credit. Lenders will access all three major credit bureaus for a score from each, and will use the middle score. For example, your credit report is requested by the mortgage company and receives three scores: 785, 763 and 751. The lender throws out the highest and lowest and uses the middle score. In this example, 763 would be the score used for qualifying.

Most lenders require a minimum credit score of 640, although there are some that go as low as 620. Lenders are fairly strict about this requirement, so if there are any credit issues, they'll need to be corrected before applying for a conventional mortgage.

Lenders will determine your affordability, and today lenders employ the ATR standard issued by the Consumer Financial Protection Bureau, or CFPB. ATR is the moniker for the Ability to Repay and among other requirements means your current monthly debt payments including the new mortgage, taxes and insurance may not exceed 43 percent of your gross monthly income.

Your income is documented differently depending upon whether or not you work for yourself or someone else. If you work for someone else, the lender will ask for your two most recent W2 forms, 1099s and your most recent paycheck stubs covering at least thirty days.

If you're self-employed, lenders will review your two most recent federal income tax returns as well as a year-to-date profit and loss statement. The main requirement for the self-employed borrower is being self-employed for at least two years. This two-year requirement is verified with your income tax returns. If you've yet to file your second year's return, you'll need to wait until it is not only filed but accepted by the IRS.

Self-employed borrowers must not only show sufficient income from the business to service the debt based upon the ATR requirement, but the income must also be consistent from year to year, with preference given to year-over-year increases. The lender will add your most recent two years' business income together, and then divide by twenty-four (months) to arrive at your qualifying income.

If, however, your year-over-year income declines, you may have trouble qualifying. Any income decrease by more than 10 to 20 percent might cause a lender to put your application on hold until the reason for the reduction in income can be reviewed. Lenders must not only verify the income but make a reasonable determination that the income will continue into the future.

Most mortgage lenders in existence today have the conventional loan in their portfolio and the approval process at least meets these guidelines. But what if there's something amiss? What if there's a lending guideline that you can't quite meet?

Portfolio lenders are traditional lenders that have no intention of selling the loan to other banks or to Fannie Mae and Freddie Mac, but intend to keep the loan in-house—in the lender's own portfolio. A portfolio is almost always a bank.

A bank can set its own internal lending parameters and make its own approvals, and as long as the guidelines are non-discriminatory a portfolio loan can be issued even if a conventional mortgage cannot. Let's look at an example of a portfolio loan coming to the rescue.

Say that a borrower makes good money as an electrician. The borrower has been in the trade for more than ten years and has a large following of satisfied clients. A year ago, the borrower decided to go out on his own and take his satisfied customers with him. He now makes more than he did working for someone else and his business does quite well, but because he doesn't have two years of income tax returns for his new business filed with the IRS he can't qualify.

A bank can easily see this and issue a loan without using the two-year requirement, though there still needs to be decent credit and a down payment.

Portfolio loans will have slightly higher interest rates compared to conventional mortgages and the loan terms may be anywhere from three to five years, but that gives the borrower enough time to establish his business, file the returns and then refinance into a conventional loan down the road.

Private Lenders

Private lenders, often referred to as "hard-money lenders," have their own internal guidelines and can approve anything they want to. What is a private lender or private money? A private lender is an individual or group of individuals who pool their funds to make loans on properties that other lenders won't make.

Private lenders look more to the exit strategy and less to traditional lending guidelines, and are important players in the real estate investment landscape. Here's a common example of what a private loan transaction would look like:

A real estate investor sees a foreclosed property that has been vacant for some time. The bank has yet to do anything with the structure, and it's in pretty bad shape. The investor brings along his contractor and inspector to the site and they all notice right away that the slab has some real issues.

In fact, the concrete foundation needs to be lifted on one side and repaired. The foundation can be fixed, but a property in such poor shape won't be eligible for a conventional or bank loan. The foundation must be repaired before a loan can be placed.

Most properties when sold will have some issues that need to be resolved between the buyer and the seller. Perhaps the hot-water heater doesn't work or the fence needs a fresh coat of paint. These are certainly items the buyer wants to have fixed, but they're not enough to keep a conventional loan from being used. The hot-water heater can easily be fixed by the seller and a fence can be painted at any time. The lender may even ignore the paint job but ask that the hot-water problem be fixed. Easy enough.

But something as significant as foundation repair or a sagging, leaking roof will stop any approval in its tracks. And there's the dilemma—the home can't be financed until the foundation is repaired, but there's no one to fix the foundation. One must come before the other.

Enter the private lender. The private lender can provide the funds to not only buy the property but also to fix the foundation and other needed repairs in order to bring the property to current standards. That way the home can be sold to almost anyone using traditional financing.

The investor makes an offer to the bank for $40,000. The contractor says the foundation repair and other work will require another $25,000. A real estate agent has done the research for the investor and determines that once the home is rehabilitated, remodeled and repainted the home could easily sell for $150,000.

The private lender sees that scenario and issues the funds. Once the home has been completed and sold, the private loan is repaid. Without private funds, millions of homes across the country could fall into a complete state of disrepair.

Private lenders make loans for riskier transactions, and as such offset that risk with more expensive terms. You can expect a down payment of at least 30 percent, interest rates in the teens and additional points and fees. The loan terms typically last only long enough to acquire, fix and sell the property. But when private lenders accept an application on a purchase, they can approve the loan and issue funds in just a few days, compared to weeks with a traditional loan.

Investor Pools

Investor pools are private funds as well, but can operate in a couple of different ways. Private investors can contribute to a lender's financing pool. The lender can then use those funds to acquire real estate investments. Investors will receive their return on their individual investment based either on an individual transaction, or on quarterly or annual profits from the lender.

You may also set up your own investor pool by having a list of private individuals ready and willing to finance your next transaction. This requires a thorough business plan that spells out how the funds will be used and how the investors will receive their profits.

As each prospective property is identified, the investor puts together a package for each investor to review. The investors can agree or decline to participate as each deal is presented.

Say that you want to buy a small strip center for $500,000, update it with an additional $200,000 and then sell it for $1.25 million. You present your business plan, provide the required data and then pool the funds together as the loan is ready to close. Individual investors may participate with whatever amount they want, say $50,000 or $100,000 each, and will receive their profits when the property is ultimately sold.

Legitimate Sources of Funds

Regardless of the loan type or the source, you'll need a down payment and funds for closing costs. Closing costs will vary depending on the location of the property, but you can expect closing costs to be around 2 to 4 percent of the sales price. Where do you get these funds?

Your lender will ask the very same question, and while the lender will certainly trust that you have enough cash in your bank account to close on the transaction, you'll be asked to provide two months of your most recent bank and investment statements.

These statements will show the ending balance of the statement period and will be the amount verified as funds to close. Any additional funds after the statement date that will be used must be verified as to the source. If you get paid on the fifteenth and thirtieth of each month, the lender will review your bank's statements and match your paycheck amounts with those listed on the bank statement.

If there are deposit discrepancies that can't be matched up with proper sources, you'll need to document the source of funds or else the lender will deduct those funds from the available balance. Even if the deposit is for a mere $200 or so, the lending guidelines require source verification.

You may also have retirement accounts that you can use. If you have a 401(k) account through your employer, you may borrow up to 50 percent of your vested interest as verified funds. If you decide to tap into a 401(k), get the process started early on, as your employer may need some time to set up the loan for you.

Do you have an IRA? Did you know that IRA funds may be used to buy and finance investment property without penalty? If an IRA of yours is self-directed, which means you are the individual responsible for determining where to invest the IRA funds, those are legitimate funds in a lender's eyes. Plus, if you sell the property the profits may be placed right back into the IRA again tax free.

It's important to note here that when using retirement funds to invest in real estate, you need to have a meeting with your financial planner or tax accountant and get a clear picture of the process and its impact on your financial plans.

Do you have an asset that can be appraised by an independent third party? A common asset might be an automobile. The year, make, model, condition and mileage of a vehicle can easily provide a value verified by an appraiser or even by comparing your car with others listed for sale. You can sell the car and use the funds to buy real estate as long as you keep a good paper trail.

I know of an investor who had a collection of rare books. The books were worth several thousand dollars but he didn't want to sell them, only borrow against them. He found a book buyer willing to loan him $15,000 with the books as collateral. The books were appraised by an independent book dealer, and because the books were an appraisable asset and the note was duly recorded and documented, the lender accepted the funds as a legitimate source.

The key? Funds may be borrowed in order to purchase real estate as long as the loan is secured. In this odd but true example, the loan was secured by the books. Just as refinancing an automobile and pulling cash out with an auto loan can be used. Even equity in other properties may be tapped into to buy real estate.

When can borrowed funds *not* be used? When the funds are unsecured, as in a credit card or personal loan. You will likely never need to secure a loan against a book collection, but sometimes a project pops up that you aren't quite ready for and you need the money quickly.

Be Prepared

Having a friend at the bank is a good idea for any business, but especially for the real estate investor. If you want to take advantage of an opportunity as it hits the market or when an owner needs to sell quickly, you shouldn't have to spend time finding out where to get your loan. Get your loan applications completed, waiting and ready at your various lending sources.

Using a conventional loan means establishing a relationship with an experienced loan officer who has a standing loan application on file. Once you sign a sales contract on a property, the loan officer simply updates your application instead of starting from scratch.

Conventional mortgages can take up to thirty days to close on a standard property due to the amount of third-party information needed, and anything you can do to shorten the time frame will help your offer.

Your hard-money lender also needs to know you. In fact, you may want to keep more than one private lender in your database. Private lenders make their own decisions, but can often form an affinity for a narrow range of projects. One private lender may specialize in rental homes, while another prefers apartment buildings or multi-unit projects.

Either way, you can expect funds more quickly from a hard money lender compared to a mortgage company or bank. Just know in advance what either will require so you can begin gathering the necessary documentation.

When you're competing with other investors or buyers in general, one thing that can help your offer stand out is being able to close quickly. Especially if the buyer has just a few days before the lender files a foreclosure notice.

The Investigation

Here's where you need to do your own fair share of due diligence. You need to make a thorough inspection of both the physical and the legal condition of the property. This is not the time to be lazy. You need to know what you're buying, so physically explore every nook and cranny to which you have access.

The legal condition refers to any current liens on the property and what might happen to those liens if the home is sold and transferred to the buyer.

What's a lien? A lien is a valid interest in a piece of real estate. An open, recorded lien means a third party in addition to the owner has a claim to the home in some fashion. There are different types of liens, but the one you're most familiar with is probably a mortgage lien.

When you obtain a home loan, your name is recorded in the public record as an owner. When you sell the home in the future, you will transfer ownership in the same fashion as you received it—with a deed. But you couldn't have received the property when you bought it unless all existing claims against the property were satisfied. If you finance a property the lender will file a lien as well. The home then cannot be transferred until the mortgage is paid off or the buyer assumes the existing mortgage with the lender's permission.

What types of liens are there besides a mortgage lien?

Mechanic's Lien. A mechanic's lien is a lien filed when a contractor begins work on a home. Major repairs to a home as well as new construction will often result in a lien being filed against the home in the amount of the contract and released when the contract is paid in full. This ensures the contractor gets paid. A mechanic's lien allows for the contractor to sue and, though subject to various state laws, can even force the sale of the home in order to get paid.

Child Support. If you owe child support, there may be a lien filed by the state or by the person receiving the support that can only be removed when the support payments end as agreed or are released by the recipient or recipient's legal guardian.

Spousal Support. Some divorce settlements require one spouse to make payments to another. The recipient may then file a lien against the home and only release it when the support payments are fulfilled.

IRS Lien. When someone fails to pay federal income tax liens as agreed, the IRS may file a lien against all real property the individual owns, including the home. Even if there are payment arrangements made with the IRS, the lien will remain until past taxes, penalties and interest are paid in full. The IRS can force the sale of the property in order to recover what is owed.

Property Tax Lien. When property taxes become delinquent, the local taxing authority has the right to file a lien against the subject property and can only be released when the taxes are paid. Depending upon where the property is located, delinquent property taxes may lead to foreclosure or a sale of the property tax lien certificate to a private investor.

Judgments. If a property owner is sued and loses a lawsuit, a court may award damages to the plaintiff. The winning party can then file a lien against personal and real property.

What do all these liens mean to a real estate investor? It means you need to understand how these liens are treated when and if a sale takes place.

If you're buying a property before a foreclosure takes place, the existing liens must be satisfied in some fashion before the home can be transferred. To find out the existence of any liens, you will need to obtain a preliminary title report from a real estate attorney or title agency in your area.

The title report will show all previous liens and when they were recorded and released, as well as any active liens, their amounts and the type of lien. If the preliminary report indicates a significant number of liens, it will take some time to get the liens verified and addressed.

Some liens may be voluntarily removed by the entity that filed the original lien, or some other arrangement may be made and the lien can be removed before or at the settlement table. However, other liens may not be so accommodating.

You can expect property taxes, the IRS, mortgage liens and home equity lines of credit (HELOCs) to remain steadfast without some sort of release or arrangement. Otherwise your lender won't place a mortgage loan on the property.

When someone is having difficulty paying the mortgage, it's highly likely they're having problems paying other bills as well. Homeowners do everything they possibly can to keep their house and will let other obligations go first before getting behind on the mortgage.

One of the reasons lenders charge higher rates for rental properties compared to an owner-occupied home is because the lender knows the rental property will go into foreclosure before the primary residence will.

The owner could have outstanding collection accounts leading to judgments. Any work done on the property might still have an outstanding mechanic's lien and property taxes, and income taxes may appear on the title report.

And if the owner can't take care of its creditors it's also likely the condition of the house has fallen into some state of disrepair because the owner can't afford to maintain the property. That's why, when possible, you need to make a visit to the home with your contractor and property inspector.

The Inspection

The preliminary title report showed the potential legal issues with the property, but you next need to determine the physical condition of the home. Your property inspector has a checklist used whenever someone orders a full inspection of a potential purchase, and this checklist will have literally hundreds of separate items to be reviewed. Each item is inspected and the inspector will note whether the item is in good condition, or needs attention or replacement. From light switches that don't work to a major electrical issue, you will find out exactly what you're getting should you purchase the property.

This needs to be done with the permission of the owner, and you may not be able to go inside the home because the home is occupied either by the owners or renters. However, if the home is already in foreclosure you may contact the lender or the agent listing the home to schedule an inspection.

You need to be on the lookout for major problems, not the minor ones. Minor issues are those that can be relatively easily repaired by you or your handyman, such as a leaky faucet or replacing the carpet. More expensive items that demand your attention include the plumbing system.

Run a pressure test on the plumbing to determine if there are any internal leaks within the system. If there are, determine the source. Leaks underneath a kitchen cabinet may be repaired, but further investigation may show that the water damage has worked its way into nearby walls and flooring. If the leak isn't obvious, then it may be coming from a broken pipe located beneath the flooring. A pier-and-beam foundation will allow your inspector to crawl underneath and possibly locate the issue, but if it's a slab foundation the leaking pipe can be a major issue.

As you work your way through the property, do you see any diagonal cracks at the top of a door jamb? Are there doors that don't close properly? That might be a sign of a foundation problem. If you suspect a foundation is bad you'll need to contact an engineer who will visit the property and locate any areas that are above or below the proper floor line.

If the house has a basement, does it smell a bit moldy? If so, it may have water issues can be difficult to remediate if you can't locate the source of the problem. Many times, it's simply an issue of making sure water flows away from the property during a rainstorm and not toward the house. Yet other issues may be cracks in the stem walls or foundation, allowing moisture to seep in.

Any spots on the ceilings? Water? Is the roof in good shape or are there missing shingles or sagging? Your inspector identifies the issues and your contractor estimates the costs of repair.

If you're working with the owner who is thinking about selling the property to you, you'll have to discover these issues on your own. Yet, when the home is listed for sale as a foreclosure, the seller is required by law to disclose any known defects or issues.

A checklist entitled the "Seller's Property Disclosure Statement" is usually available to assist the seller. This form lists any issues that the seller knows or should know about the property. Perhaps there was an area that flooded during a strong thunderstorm or the roof leaked. Maybe the hot-water heater doesn't heat very well. Whatever issue there may be, the seller is required to tell you about it in advance.

Many times, however, the seller lists the property "as is" and you don't get to inspect the home. Or the seller does know about certain issues and has made you aware of them, but will not fix them. That will be up to you, the buyer.

The utilities may also be disconnected, so you won't be able to determine if there are any electrical, plumbing or gas problems. Inspecting the property may not be an opportunity for you so you'll be investing in a home without fully knowing its true condition. Your offer should reflect that risk.

Bidding Like a Pro

So it's time for your first auction. You've already visited the county recorder's office or visited their website to get a list of properties that will be auctioned off. You've reviewed the title report and found out as much as you can about the physical condition of the home, and now it's time to walk the talk. What can you expect at an auction?

If you've never attended an auction before, it's good advice to attend your first with no intention of making any bid. You're there to observe. At any large public auction, whether it's for a rare piece of artwork or a classic automobile, there is no shortage of gamesmanship. Some bidders may be loud, others will bid with the tip of a hat and some will wait till just seconds before the gavel falls as the auctioneer says, "Going once . . . going twice . . ." and then another bid pops up just when someone else thinks they've won the property.

Auctioneers are good at what they do, and their primary goal is to get the highest price possible. It's easy to get caught up in the frenzy, so don't lose your head. Attend your first auction as an observer, not a buyer.

On the other hand, an auction may be much more subdued, and held at an attorney's office with just a few people attending.

The first step in the bidding process is determining the maximum amount you're willing to pay. With your real estate agent, determine what the property would be worth in good condition. If you sell the home, will the sales price be enough to cover your selling expenses in addition to the amount you paid for it? If there's one thing to keep in mind at all times it is this: don't let emotions make business decisions for you. The numbers must work or there's no deal. Remember, you're a real estate investor, not a speculator.

If you don't intend to sell the property but wish to keep it for the long term and rent it out for monthly cash flow in addition to property appreciation, your real estate agent can provide you with a proper market rent for the home. However, if you decide to dispose of the property, keep your magic number at the forefront.

There will be times when you break your own rule and bid $100,100 on a property that you figured you'd pay no more than $100,000 for. You can do that once, or maybe twice. But if you're continually being bid up, your profit margins will shrink, and if you don't watch out, you'll be doing nothing more than breaking even. Or worse. You can't "wish" a property value into being. Follow the advice given to you by your agent.

We'll go into more detail later in the book about how to calculate a maximum price. Just don't let the auction get too overheated.

Pay close attention to the auctioneer, and if you hear a phrase something like "Property being sold subject to all existing liens," that means the successful bidder is responsible for any valid liens that currently exist on the property, such as mechanic's liens or IRS liens. If you reviewed the title report ahead of time on a property you're interested in and it still makes sense at a certain price, that's okay, but if you haven't, beware.

Know in advance what the payment procedure is. Some areas ask for a cash deposit, and then allow you twenty-four hours to come up with the difference in the form of a cashier's check. You won't have time to arrange financing. Do you remember what I said earlier in the book about how you can learn from my mistakes and avoid them? Let me share something that shows you exactly what I mean.

It was back in 2011, and I had been buying more foreclosures than anyone else in Arizona—approximately two hundred per month at that time. In Arizona, when you're the successful bidder, you can place a cash deposit, and then have until the end of the next business day to come up with the rest.

At that time, we thought we'd take our business model to California, and we opened up an office in Orange County. In California, though, we didn't have twenty-four hours. We had to come up with the funds right then and there. We did, but it wasn't exactly pocket change.

We used the same firms we used in Arizona for title examination and figured that the process was the same in California. We first bought a batch of foreclosed properties and made about $240,000 on the transaction. We then bought even more homes, but lost $100,000. Why?

Things change so rapidly in this business. At the time we relied on a tax credit that helped spur home buying. But the credit went away and we weren't prepared for the slowdown. We knew about the tax-credit expiration, but had no idea about the impact. We were wrong and we lost money. Since we guarantee a return to our clients, we paid the difference to our clients who provided the investment funds. Not our best day.

In another instance, we bought a property for $280,000 that was worth maybe $450,000. However there was an existing $500,000 first mortgage on the property, and we almost lost everything. Fortunately, my relationship with those involved let us rescind our deal. Real estate is real money and it's not the most liquid investment around.

You have to be clear in your mind what you're going to pay, how and when you're going to pay for it and what you're going to do with it and when. If you don't know the answers to all of those questions, you'll be in a position you don't want to be in.

Finally, know where you're bidding in addition to what you're bidding on. There are foreclosure services online that let you bid on properties from the comfort of your own home or office ten states away. Would you bid on such a property? Maybe if you were playing with Monopoly money, but not with real cash.

Instead, become a specialist in a particular area. You know where the schools are. You know the neighborhoods and proximity to shopping, dining and thoroughfares, and you will ultimately know what homes are selling and renting for like the back of your hand. You can't find out enough about a potential property. Take your time, do your homework and keep a steady hand.

CHAPTER 6
Wholesales, Short Sales and Strategies

When buying investment property, whether it's for a flip or a long-term hold, you have an opportunity to acquire a property at various stages of the foreclosure process. I've discussed that process at length, but I want to elaborate on two strategies that successful real estate investors use every day when a home has yet to be foreclosed upon: wholesales and short sales. You may have heard the terms before but were not quite sure exactly how they work in the real world.

Wholesaling

If you've heard the late-night clamor of "Make millions investing in real estate with no money down, bad credit and even no job whatsoever!" or some such claim, you can bet they're talking about wholesaling real estate. In essence, that claim is true, but it's far from a get-rich scheme. It takes work, talent and perseverance to be a successful wholesaler. I know: I'm one of them. But it's time to change the channel and get a real-world explanation of what wholesaling really is and how to profit from it.

What is wholesaling? Like any product, wholesaling means buying at a lower price, below retail, and selling for a higher price, at retail. That's basically how any industry sells a product.

A manufacturer will build a hundred widgets, and then sell those widgets to various distributors throughout the country. The distributors have a customer base that likes to buy widgets. The distributor marks up the price of the widget to retail level.

The very same process is applied to real estate. An investor—you—finds a property in a distressed situation, and the owner needs to sell quickly. You make an offer below market, and then assign the sales contract to an investor from your database, who agrees to purchase the subject property from you at a higher price.

Here's an example of a typical wholesale transaction.

You find a property that with some work would sell for $100,000, but the value is nowhere near that amount. You determine that the property needs another $15,000 of work before it can be sold for $100,000. You make an offer to the seller for $60,000. The owner accepts and you both sign the sales contract. This is where the wholesaling begins.

The "no money from your pocket" part starts here. Most wholesale transactions don't have an earnest money deposit, an amount from you held by a third party, the escrow officer or settlement agent. The owner may not accept a sales contract without any earnest money so you may be required to make such a deposit, but make it a marginal one, say $500.

Your offer to the owner will also include language that allows you to assign the contract to a third party, who will be one of your investors. Your signature on the sales contract will have an assignee clause that reads something to the effect of "Doug Hopkins or his successors or assigns," which allows you to transfer the sales contract.

Next, you assign the contract to your investor at the price you and your investor have agreed upon. In this example, you agree to assign the contract for $70,000. Your investor proceeds with the sale for $70,000 at the closing table. You have just made $10,000 as a wholesaler and your investor still has an attractive investment.

That is the basic process of wholesaling. Now let's talk a little bit about some of the finer points of the process.

The most important component of wholesaling is a database of clients who will buy what you have to sell. Without a cadre of confident investors, you'll never reach the retail part of the equation. This means you need to validate your database and get to know the investors on your list, their preferences and price ranges. What are some of the things you need to know about a potential investor?

The first is the price range of the investment. You need to know what the investor will feel comfortable buying and whether or not the investor is a cash buyer or will need to finance the acquisition.

You want to find as many cash buyers as possible because one of the primary motives of a distressed owner is to sell as quickly as possible, most often to avoid a foreclosure or just after an NOD.

You should also have at least one hard-money contact to refer your buyer to if they don't have or aren't willing to put up cash in such a very short period of time.

Next, what types of property does the investor prefer? Single-family homes? Duplexes? What neighborhood do you feel comfortable investing in? Are there any areas you'd like to avoid? And finally, what is your appetite? Using the investor's parameters, how many homes per year would the investor like to buy?

You can't have enough investors, and you should constantly cultivate more of them. What are some ways to find investors? If you recall how bird dogs find leads, then you'll appreciate how to find investors to whom you can assign contracts.

Remember that investors use bandit signs to find owners who are about to be foreclosed upon or otherwise need to sell quickly. You want those who can buy quickly and pay cash. Instead of a sign saying "Cash Buyers for Your House!" your handwritten bandit sign should read "Need to sell fast! Cash buyers only!" Your marketing is now in reverse: instead of looking for sellers, you're looking for cash buyers.

When you get a contract on a property, whether for a wholesale transaction or a standard purchase, place bandit signs throughout the neighborhood where the subject property is located. Response calls will be an investor or someone who has access to a cash buyer.

Your real estate agent can help you to find both properties to wholesale and cash buyers. Most multiple-listing services show how a recent sale was financed or if it was a cash sale. If cash, is the property now listed as a rental? If so, then you've identified a cash investor. You can do the very same with any home listed as a rental.

Contact the owner and mention that you're a wholesaler. Ask if the investor would like to review any future deals. There's a new investor to add to your database.

That's how wholesaling works and where the part about "no money, no credit" comes into play. An earnest money deposit may not always be needed, but if the seller insists, keep it relatively small. You'll get your deposit back when the deal closes, in addition to your profit. No credit is needed because you're not applying for a loan; you're simply putting a home under contract, and then finding an investor to assign the contract to at a higher price. Lenders aren't involved.

Many real estate investors start out as wholesalers. It involves much of the evaluation process that investors employ without funds needed from you.

Short Sales

Short sales are another offshoot of the real estate bust that started in the previous decade. A short sale occurs when a lender agrees to accept less than what is owed on the property as "paid in full." Short sales are not a new phenomenon. They have been an option for homeowners who fall into financial trouble for as long as there have been lenders. It's just not something that banks or mortgage companies advertise.

When a property owner begins having problems making the mortgage payments on a consistent basis, the lender and the borrower will typically first explore a loan repayment plan. The bank will take the past due amounts, and then spread the delinquent funds over a six- or twelve-month period.

The borrower continues to make regular mortgage payments, with an additional amount to be applied to the outstanding mortgage payments.

A borrower may also have the option of a loan modification. A loan modification is a process in which the lender modifies some feature of the existing note, usually the interest rate on the mortgage, to lower the monthly payment.

In both scenarios the borrower will complete an application for the lender to review. Lenders will validate the gross monthly income, and then adjust the interest rate to accommodate the income. This means pay check stubs and bank statements, along with a thorough review of the borrowers' current financial status.

It's very possible that the interest rate cannot be lowered enough to qualify the owner for the repayment plan or modification. In fact, there may be no income at all, and neither a repayment plan nor loan modification can take place. The only apparent option is a foreclosure.

Unless the owner can apply for and successfully negotiate a short sale.

If the owner can sell a home quickly for cash to avoid foreclosure, he will. And hopefully he will sell it to you. But selling a property requires a minimum amount of equity, otherwise the seller must come up with thousands in order to close on a sale. If the owner had that sort of cash, it's likely he wouldn't be in a potential foreclosure situation.

For example, a property owner purchases a single-family home in 2008 for $500,000, puts 10 percent down and finances the remaining $450,000. Pretty much at the wrong time, but the owner bought the home for the long term and not for a flip. Over the years, however, the property value fell dramatically, and five years later the mortgage was paid down to less than $415,000. However, the property value of the home fell to $300,000. On its own that's not a problem. But now the owner falls upon hard times and has been unemployed for six months and can no longer afford the payments.

The owner desperately needs to sell, but in order for a sale to take place, the owner would be forced to come to the closing with the difference between the current market value of $300,000 and the outstanding loan balance of $415,000. That's $115,000 the owner has to come up with before getting out from under the mortgage and facing a foreclosure.

Enter the short sale.

You make an offer on the property at a price just below market value. In this example, say $270,000. You write up a sales contract and you and the owner agree to it. The owner, not you, then makes a request the lender to accept a short sale offer. Why would the bank consider such an option?

Lenders entertain short sale requests because the loss would be greater if they foreclosed. If the bank foreclosed on this transaction, they pay additional legal fees, lost interest and penalties, and then put the home up for auction and most likely end up selling the property for much less than your short sale offer.

In order for the short sale to be accepted, the bank needs to be convinced a foreclosure can't be avoided any other way. When a property owner applies for a short sale approval, the owner will present to the lender:

- Most recent paycheck stubs (if any)
- Explanation letter for the current situation
- Bank and investment statements verifying current assets
- A signed sales contract with a specific price
- A property appraisal providing comparable sales for the area and a current market valuation of the home

Note that the loan must be delinquent, typically anywhere from sixty to ninety days or more, with a pattern of late payments and no evidence of the ability to correct the borrower's situation.

Upon review of the short sale request, the lender can then decide whether or not to accept the offer. Unfortunately, a short sale request adds time to the approval process and a short sale evaluation could take sixty days or longer, although lenders who have approved thousands of short sales have improved their processing times.

You need to be prepared going into a short sale and have your financing or cash lined up prior to making the offer. Include a copy of either your approval letter from your lender or check the box marked "Cash Sale."

A short sale is truly a win-win-win scenario. The owner gets out from under a mortgage he can no longer afford and a foreclosure stays off of a credit report. The bank wins by losing less than it otherwise would have, and you win because you've purchased a property at a price below market.

Either situation, wholesaling or a short sale, means the property has yet to go into foreclosure, or if it has the lender is still working with the owner to get the problem remediated. To approach either scenario, remember to first explore county records for a notice of default or foreclosure filing.

CHAPTER 7
Buying and Holding

Much of the attention in recent years was given to the investment strategy of flipping. Flipping is where an investor buys, rehabs and then sells a property within a short period of time, usually less than six months. While that's a lucrative market, I would rather buy and hold an investment for the long term if the project makes sense.

Longer term investments provide me with a steady cash flow from the unit each month. Where the market has been, what I paid for the property and where I think the market will go will also provide me and my family with additional equity over the years. Let's talk about how to evaluate a property for a long-term hold.

What is the most important thing to know regarding rental properties? It has to cash flow each month. The rental payments must exceed not only the mortgage payment, but the associated expenses as well. Before we get to cash flow, we need to determine our financing costs, and as we mentioned back in Chapter 5, the best financing for an investor property is a conventional loan, the most common mortgage program in the market today.

The sales price on the property has to be as low as you can get it, but there may also be repairs that you'll need to consider. You can finance the mortgage, but few mortgage programs offer any significant funds for repairs for investment properties. That means you'll need a down payment between 20 and 25 percent, plus funds for repairs.

The Mortgage Payment

Your mortgage payment is calculated based upon the loan amount, the interest rate and the term of the loan. The loan amount and the loan term is something you can control, the interest rate not so much. Your loan amount will be 75 to 80 percent of the final sales price.

Let's look at an example. A home is listed at $150,000 and needs only minor repairs, such as interior paint and a thorough cleaning.

Sales Price	$150,000
Down Payment	$30,000
Loan Amount	$120,000

Your loan amount is $120,000, and using a thirty-year fixed rate at, say, 5 percent, the principal and interest payment is $644. But you must also allow for annual property taxes and insurance. If property taxes are $1,500 per year and homeowner's insurance $750 per year, by dividing those amounts by twelve (months) you'll break down the tax and insurance expense into a monthly amount. Your monthly payment now looks like this:

P&I	$644
Taxes	$125
Insurance	$63
Total PITI	$832

As long as the monthly rent exceeds $832 you've got a positive cash flow. But don't forget about maintenance costs. A hot-water heater may go out or a plumber may need to visit the property to unplug a drain. You should count on an additional 10 percent of the rent for maintenance.

If you charge $1,500 in rent, you should add an additional $150 to your cash flow calculation, which would make your monthly expense $832 + $150 = $982. You'll get a better feel for maintenance charges as you acquire more properties, but the age of the home and the condition of the property will give you guidance on what to expect year over year in hard maintenance costs.

In this example with a $1,500 rent, you're making $518 each month. Not bad. But what if your repair costs came in at $8,000? You need to make that up, right? By dividing $8,000 by $518 you'll get the costs of repairs back in just over fifteen months.

We mentioned earlier that you have the choice of the loan amount. That's because you agreed to a specific sales price and chose to put down 20 percent. You also have a choice of the loan term. What types of loan terms are available?

Conventional mortgages have loan terms as short as ten years, and up to thirty years in five-year increments. While most people know that they can get a fifteen- or a thirty-year mortgage, they may not know that there are also twenty- and twenty-five-year options. Which is best?

The longer the loan term, the lower the monthly payment and the shorter the term, the higher the payment. The difference is not just in the monthly payment but how much interest is paid over the life of the loan. Shorter terms require less interest to the lender.

For example, consider a $200,000 loan amount with a 4.50 and 4.00 respective rate:

Term	Rate	Payment
30 yr	4.50	$1,013
15 yr	4.00	$1,479

So why doesn't everyone just pick the thirty-year loan, since it's so much lower? Let's now look at the interest paid on each loan taken to term:

Term	Rate	Payment	Interest
30 yr	4.50	$1,013	$164,680
15 yr	4.00	$1,479	$66,220

That's why. The fifteen-year loan not only pays off twice as fast, but in this example saves nearly $100,000 in interest expense. If you want to save on interest but the fifteen-year payment is too high, lenders also offer twenty- and twenty-five-year loans.

Here's that same example with the additional choices:

Term	Rate	Payment	Interest
30 yr	4.50	$1,013	$164,680
25 yr	4.50	$1,111	$133,499
20 yr	4.00	$1,211	$ 90,870
15 yr	4.00	$1,479	$ 66,220

Most investors like to have the lowest payment, which is accomplished with the thirty-year loan. Since conventional mortgages don't have prepayment penalties, you can always make an extra payment or two each year to reduce your long-term interest costs, so remember you have options.

Finally, you don't have control over your interest rate. At least until you lock that rate in. Mortgage rates can change daily, and even throughout the course of any trading day. This will determine how much you'll make each month—if anything.

You can get general rate quotes from your lender, but remember your interest rate is not guaranteed until you specifically instruct your lender to lock you in. Mortgage rates are tied to a specific index and are used each business day when lenders establish mortgage rates for their customers. To lock in an interest rate, your lender will require that you have a completed application on file.

Officially, a completed application includes all your personal information, such as who you are, where you work and how much money you have available to close on the purchase. A property must also be selected. If any one of these bits of information is missing, your lender may refuse your lock request.

Generally, the shorter the lock term the cheaper the rate will be. Most lenders quote rates in thirty-day increments. For instance, a lender might quote 5 percent with no points for a thirty-day guarantee, or 5 percent with one point for a sixty-day lock. One point equals one percent of the amount borrowed.

Most closings will occur within a thirty-day period, so longer term locks are usually not required. All that said, it is up to you to make the final determination on the rate and whether or not to pay points.

Should you pay points, called "discount" points, to get a lower rate? Maybe, but usually the math doesn't work out. Lenders don't really care if you pay a point or not, because the lender ultimately gets the same amount of interest. Usually one point on a thirty-year loan reduces your rate by .25 percent. If you can get a 5 percent rate with no points, you might be able to secure 4.75 with one point. Let's look again at a $200,000 loan amount.

If 5 percent on $200,000 is $1,073, then 4.75 would give a $1,043 payment, or $30 lower. But you paid one point, or $2,000 for the lower rate. If you divide $2,000 by $30 you get 67 (months). That's how long it takes in this example to recover the point. Every scenario will be slightly different, but the math will always guide you. Again, the lender is indifferent.

Broker or Banker?

Conventional mortgages for real estate investors are available at most residential mortgage companies in the United States. While you may have nailed down the type of loan you want, where do you get the mortgage? There are two primary sources for mortgage loans for investors in the United States: mortgage brokers and mortgage bankers. Who are they and what are the differences?

A mortgage broker is a person or entity, not a lender, that arranges financing between the borrower and the ultimate lender. It is similar to an independent insurance agent who represents multiple insurance companies. Brokers don't approve the loans; they find loans that match up with the borrower's profile.

Brokers have business arrangements with mortgage companies that operate a "wholesale" division. Wholesale lenders find mortgage brokers who can bring in mortgage loans. The mortgage broker sets up shop, hires loan officers, rents space, buys computers and provides all the overhead needed for a loan officer to generate business.

In exchange for the broker taking on the expense of originating mortgage loans, wholesale lenders offer rates to brokers below market level. The broker then "marks up" the rate in order to compete at a retail level.

A mortgage broker can work with multiple lenders and can have the ability to shop around for the best mortgage rate by comparing lenders on your behalf. In the case of an investor, those programs will almost always consist of conventional loans underwritten to Fannie Mae or Freddie Mac guidelines. In theory, a broker can review wholesale rate offers from ten different wholesale lenders to find the best price.

Once found, the broker sends the loan application, along with your documentation, to the wholesale lender to complete the approval process. Your loan will be underwritten by the wholesale lender and your loan papers will have the name of the lender on them, not the name of the broker.

Historically, brokers commanded as much as two-thirds of the loan origination market, primarily due to their ability to market different types of mortgage loans. This meant that someone with terrible credit could get a subprime loan through a mortgage broker. Perhaps a borrower couldn't prove income or assets, even though they had them. The broker might find a lender who provided "alternative" loan programs.

However, with the mortgage meltdown in the last decade those loan programs are long gone and today are controlled by Fannie and Freddie loans. That said, a mortgage broker's utility has been compromised as a broker offers the same suite of mortgage loans that other lenders have.

And at the same time, since mortgage companies all set their interest rates on the same indices, mortgage rates shouldn't vary all that much from one lender to the next. There are differences, but not as dramatic as they used to be.

What does a mortgage banker do? A mortgage banker is responsible for originating, processing, documenting, approving and funding a mortgage application. The loan doesn't have to be sent to yet another lender for an approval as everything is performed in-house.

A mortgage banker typically sells all its loans to other lenders or directly to Fannie Mae or Freddie Mac, and is the primary source of revenue for the lender, along with lender fees and underwriting charges. A mortgage banker does not have different lenders from which to choose the best rate, but can decide who to sell the loan to in advance from a list of lenders.

In today's lending environment, there really isn't a lot of difference between a broker and a banker, and both have the same group of mortgage products. One difference, however, refers to what lenders call "overlays."

An overlay is an additional lending guideline imposed on a mortgage program, but that still meets conventional lending requirements. For example, a Fannie Mae loan program might require a credit score of 640 for an investor property loan, but the individual lender decides to make the minimum higher, say 660 or 670. The loan is still eligible for sale in the secondary markets because the score meets the conventional guideline; it's just a little more difficult to qualify for.

A mortgage broker will have a list of overlays that different lenders impose. If one lender requires a 660 score, the broker may know of another lender needing only a 640 and can send the loan application to the wholesale lender allowing for the lower score.

Increasingly, however, mortgage bankers also have lenders to sell the loan to that operate under the same format and different overlays.

So which is the better choice, a broker or a banker? In my opinion, it really doesn't matter as long as the loan closes on time and the rates are competitive. Maybe the difference is that the broker loses control over the loan once it is submitted to the wholesale lender. I've used brokers, banks and mortgage bankers and in today's lending environment the only real difference is the process.

The most important thing you can do is to establish a relationship with at least two mortgage companies and be loyal to them. If they continue to provide you with excellent customer service and take care of you, it's important that you return the favor. Don't shop around each acquisition to multiple lenders. You need one on your side at all times.

Getting Approved the Second Time Around

In Chapter 5 we discussed the approval process regarding income and credit requirements, but something rather magical happens after you buy your first property. It gets easier to qualify . . . much easier.

When you buy and finance your first unit to be held as a rental, you'll have to qualify based upon your current household income. The rental income can't be used even though you can prove it's there with a rental agreement and copies of cancelled checks. It might be disheartening at first, but take heart because it gets better.

When real estate investors buy their first property they see their decision play out in real life. There is a mortgage but the rent that comes in more than pays for the costs of holding the property. It's nothing less than someone paying you to buy real estate. Not only do you enjoy the monthly income, but the property is appreciating at the same time. That motivates the first-time investor to become a second- and third-time investor. But can the investor afford to carry two and three more home loans?

Conventional lenders allow rental income to be used to offset the new mortgage payment as long as the investor can document at least two years' experience being a landlord. How can you prove it?

You can prove it with a copy of your credit report showing mortgage loans and your two most recent federal income tax returns with Schedule E attached. Schedule E is where you list your rental income, expenses, depreciation and associated costs. If you've got two years of Schedule E, lenders will begin counting rental income.

Now all you need to do is provide your down payment along with supporting documentation and rental income can be counted. That's when many investors suddenly add multiple properties to their portfolios, because there's no longer the need to carry the full load of the new mortgage payment.

The two-year landlord requirement is in place to make sure you have the experience needed to properly manage your real estate assets. It is much like a self-employed borrower who must have at least two years on the job before a lender will approve a mortgage loan application.

Get past the first one, and in two years' time it's easy. Note that different lenders can insert their own overlays and restrict how many financed properties you may own at one time, but the two-year hurdle is a point in time that all investors will remember.

Market Rents

Okay, you've figured out what the mortgage payment plus associated costs will be, but will it cash flow? That's relatively easy to find out simply by asking the tenants what they pay each month in rent. If there are no tenants in the subject property, you might find other rental properties in the area for more information. However, you may find that someone renting will be not all that enthusiastic about telling you how much they're paying each month to live there.

Of course, you can always call the property owner, and then compare that property with yours. The local MLS will also have a list of homes for rent and how much the rent will be. You want a competitive rent, but you also want to make as much as you can.

You'll be able to get a good feel for current market rents for a property like yours, but if you want a more detailed report you can contact your appraiser and ask for a market rent survey.

For a couple of hundred dollars, your appraiser will provide you with a number that you can feel comfortable charging. If you make a mistake and charge a little less than you could have, remember your lease agreement will come up for renewal and you can reevaluate your position at that time.

What Makes a Good Landlord? Good Tenants

Good tenants are really the secret when you're a landlord. You want someone that pays on time, takes care of the property and is very low maintenance. And by taking a few simple steps, you can find tenants who will tick all three boxes for you. You will have maintenance problems every now and then, but you don't want to be chasing down rent each month or, worse, having to evict.

When qualifying a potential renter, you need to think like a bank. You want to make sure they can afford your rent comfortably and have demonstrated a responsible credit history. Both of these investigations will get you well on the way to snagging the best tenants.

Your lease application should also include an authorization form that allows you to check on the applicant's credit, rental history, employment and the character of all adult occupants. This is important, because sometimes there will be three or four adults living in the same unit, and if two move out you can't hold them responsible for rent payments if they're not on the lease.

When occupancy changes and fewer renters are living in your unit during the course of the lease, the sudden loss of income can cause the remaining occupants to struggle with the payment. You don't have any rights as a landlord if you don't have all legal occupants on the lease.

When banks evaluate a mortgage application, they first verify the gross monthly income of all who will be on the application. The rent should be somewhere near one-third of that amount. So, if gross monthly income is $3,000 then a comfortable rent payment would be $1,000, and so on.

In addition to rent, you need to look at any other credit obligations, such as an auto loan, credit card or student loan payment. By looking at a credit report, you can determine if there are any additional payments, and if so the amount of the minimum due. When you add up the housing payment with other credit obligations, banks like that number to be no more than 40 percent of gross income.

How do you verify income? Ask for two copies of their most recent paycheck stubs covering at least thirty days. At the same time, contact their employers and verify they work there.

There's no need to get an income verification, but with the proper authorization form you can. In fact, all you may need to do is call the employer and ask for the prospective tenant by name. If you get transferred to the right extension, you've verified employment.

Next, verify the credit report. Don't rely on a credit report supplied by the prospective tenants; retrieve one on your own for all renters on the application. There are multiple online sources for landlords to pull an independent credit report when evaluating credit.

When reviewing the report, you should see various trade lines, which will include the creditor, the original amount owed, current balance, minimum monthly payment and if there have been any payments that are more than thirty, sixty and ninety days late.

Truly delinquent accounts will show as "collection," and at some point the creditor gives up trying to collect from the borrower and sends the matter to court. Once the court has awarded damages to the creditor, you will see the word "judgment" listed as a public record, along with an account that was "charged off" as uncollectible.

You don't want any accounts in such a status. You want current credit accounts paid on time, with no lates. There may be times when there are in fact late payments listed on the report, but if the late payments are few and sporadic that's not much of an issue. Also pay close attention to the amount of credit available compared to credit lines allowed. Why?

Say there are two applicants who have three credit cards open, each with a $5,000 credit limit. One applicant has a $500 balance on each card, for a total of $1,500. The other applicant has two balances of $4,700, and the third is actually over the credit line, at $5,200.

Now, who has the better credit? That's easy: it's the applicant with the lower balances. Don't just look for late payments; look to see if the applicant has been using lots of credit as of late. This could be an early indicator of potential credit problems.

Now take the minimum amounts due, add the monthly rent and then compare that with the gross monthly income. Is it within range? Is the rent payment one-third of gross income and all credit around 40 percent? If so, you can expect timely rent payments. By contacting the previous landlord you can get an idea of the type of tenants you'll be leasing to.

Be somewhat guarded, though, when speaking with a current landlord. It's always possible the landlord can provide a glowing report, only to get rid of the tenants as soon as possible. And finally, drive by the applicant's current address just to take a look at where they live. What is the condition of the property? Is the yard kept? Front porch cleared of debris? Overall, does it appear the current tenants are taking care of the rental?

If you've done all this legwork, you've found a good tenant. And once found, lock them up for a year, and if they're as good as you originally thought, a few months before the lease expires, you may want to approach them to sign a longer term lease just to keep those marvelous tenants.

If they're not as good as advertised, then you have the option of increasing the rent to offset any problems, or refusing to renew and looking for new tenants. Renters rarely stay in one place for very long. A two-year lease is usually the exception and not the rule, so understand that finding and maintaining tenants is an ongoing process. Especially if you have multiple properties.

Property-Management Firms

Let's say you've got two nice rental properties and some nice tenants to go along with them. It's a Sunday afternoon and you're on the golf course with your buddies, getting ready to tee off on number eleven. Just on your buddy's backswing, your mobile phone begins to buzz. You look down and recognize that it's one of your tenants. Calling on a Sunday afternoon.

"Hey, sorry to bother you but the toilet and bathtub in the downstairs bathroom are backing up and there's black stuff all over the place. Water's leaking out of the door down into the basement!"

What do you do? If you had a property management firm, you would never have received that call. You'd be getting ready to pull out your driver and tee off on the next hole.

Property-management firms take care of the day-to-day activities of your rental properties, and can take on as little or as much as you'd like to hand off. Property managers can hold an open house, list your rental and accept rental applications. Property managers vet the applicants by reviewing a credit report, verifying employment, taking deposits, mowing the yard, and collecting the monthly rent. If tenants get behind on the rent, the property manager starts making collection calls and picks up the past-due amounts for you.

If the bathroom tub starts to back up and the toilet is leaking into the basement, the property manager contacts a plumber for you and has the matter resolved. Does that sound like something you'd be interested in hearing more about?

Property managers take on the mundane tasks of real estate investing and let you enjoy the fun parts: making money and watching your portfolio grow. But they don't do it for free. Property managers will charge a percentage of the rent collected each month, which will be based upon the services you choose.

Property managers can be independent firms who manage small, single-family homes to large, multi-unit apartment buildings. They're easy to find, and one of the first places you might start is with a real estate agency. Most large real estate firms have an internal property-management division, and it's very likely that the agent you regularly work with also has access to a property manager at their brokerage.

If you are satisfied with just one or maybe two rentals, a property manager may not be something you think you need, but it really is a matter of personal preference. And when you start collecting several rental properties, you'll soon wonder how you lived without the services of a property manager.

CHAPTER 8
Team Building

Early on in this book I pointed out that investing in real estate makes more money for more people than any other industry, and you don't need a college degree or millions of dollars in the bank. But the industry has so many moving parts that it's hard to keep up with them all, especially if you're just starting out.

If a mistake is made, you'll have to overcome it. However, you shouldn't travel your real estate journey alone—you need to surround yourself with experts who will help you along the way and contribute to your success.

When first starting out you won't have very many people around you. It may be that you've found your first property on your own and today it's rented out without any issues whatsoever. And that's how it should be. Yet as you acquire more real estate, plates start to spin and you'll need some help. What is a team and who should be on it?

Your team consists of real estate industry experts who play some part or provide a service each time a property is sold. You will be surprised at how many different players are involved. Some are relatively important while some are critical. Let's start putting your team together.

Real Estate Agent

Perhaps the most important team member of them all is your real estate agent. Your agent will be involved in every single transaction you're involved in. You don't need an agent simply to make an offer on a home; your agent will also be able to provide you with valuable insight on the real estate market and neighborhoods that provide opportunities, and will help establish the buy and sell price.

You want the best agent you can find, and you may in fact go through more than one agent before you find the right fit, but you shouldn't go it alone without an agent.

Your real estate agent has a vested interest in your success as an investor. Each time your agent makes an offer on your behalf and successfully negotiates a contract, the agent makes a commission that's paid for by the seller.

The agent will also market your property once you've acquired it, and will find buyers during the rehab or hold an open house when the home is ready to show. When your agent sells your flip or rents out one of your units, the agent earns another commission. Once you begin to show that you're serious about this business you'll find that you have a dedicated professional at your service.

A professional real estate agent knows neighborhood trends. That's a key ingredient when deciding whether or not to buy in a particular area. If a home goes up for sale either by a private seller, through a bank or listed by another broker, your agent can provide you with data that helps you determine whether or not the investment makes sense, if the price is too high or the price is so low that you have to jump on it right away or miss out. The agent gets paid on both ends of the deal and that will earn a lot of loyalty.

Say that your agent brings a potential deal for you to review. Your agent will have already reviewed the asking price, what improvements could be added and what the home would sell for once completed, or they will have compared rental rates in the area to determine if the property will cash flow.

It's a nice package to receive. All you need to do is evaluate the proposal, perform your own due diligence and determine whether or not to proceed. So, how do you find a good agent?

Everyone in any business is a rookie out of the starting gate. There are probably some very promising if not already productive real estate newbies who will one day make a lot of money. Though you might very well recruit a newbie to bird dog some properties for you, you want a professional for the long term. You want someone who is not only excellent at evaluating buy/ sell prices, but who has earned a reputation in the industry as one of the best. That agent is trusted, and has established a profile that can only be earned through action and not slick advertisements.

A top agent is one who has plenty of listings. Your brother-in-law may have his real estate license and is eager to act as your agent, but he may only do real estate part time. After all, he's really an accountant.

Get referrals from friends and colleagues for agents they have used. You can also drive around neighborhoods you're interested in, looking for "For Sale" or "For Rent" signs. Check whose name is at the bottom of the sign. If you see that one agent has many more listings than others, then you've got a great starting point.

You can do the same when you log on to a real estate website and see who has the most listings. Any agent that has been around for a while and has ten listings on a website must have a good reputation.

Caution here, though: real estate sites may also pull listing information directly from the MLS, and a listing may appear to be coming from one agent when in fact it's listed by another firm entirely.

Gather a few names of real estate agents and ask that they meet with you. Tell each agent that you're looking to buy a rental property and are interviewing local agents to help find your first property. Emphasize "first" so they understand that this first purchase won't be your last.

When the agents meet with you one by one, you should expect a professional package that highlights the agent's accomplishments, how they'll find what you're looking for and anything else the agent can bring to the table. At this stage, you've narrowed your choices to maybe three or four agents, and it now comes down to nothing more than personality.

Who do you feel comfortable with? Do your personalities gel or is there something that just doesn't feel right? For example, a very successful agent might be a solid "Type A" personality, but you're not comfortable with that trait. Instead, you may be looking for someone more collaborative, someone that you feel comfortable with.

Communication is so important at this level that it can't be overemphasized. When an agent brings you a deal it's you who decides whether or not to proceed. Don't feel intimidated or pushed into any decision. You have to feel comfortable with your agent and know that you two can communicate with one another freely and nobody gets their feelings hurt. Your new agent is now your new best friend.

Contractor

You may be pretty handy around the house. You know how to replace a sink disposal and you know what Teflon tape is for, but when you're talking about a few thousand dollars that can make or break a potential investment, you need someone who knows how to fix what needs fixing, how long repairs will take and, most important, the costs involved.

Say that your agent brings you a potential deal and you plan an on-site visit to the property. If you're involved in a short sale, the owner will be more than happy to let you and your contractor stop by for an inspection. Your offer is contingent upon an inspection.

The contractor can tell you what needs to be done to the property, if anything. For example, you may visit a unit and find out that it needs very little work, other than a few cosmetic repairs such as paint and steam cleaning the carpet.

But the contractor also notices a tiny crack just above one of the door jambs, and that the door has to be pushed slightly before it shuts completely. You may not notice such a crack, but your contractor will. Suddenly a home that you thought required just a few hundred dollars of TLC might need some major repairs.

Another property hits your radar, and you and your contractor again make a joint appearance. You notice immediately that there are several shingles missing. The driveway is cracked and uneven and the back wooden deck is in complete disrepair.

Your contractor makes a note of all that needs attention and tells you that the new roof will cost around $3,000, the driveway is not much of a problem and a simple power wash will do, but the back deck will need to be replaced. You can save some money by using pavers instead of new wood, so the contractor provides you with options.

After you've determined how much the repairs will cost and how much it will take to make the home ready for showing you call your real estate agent to ask what the home would sell for once all the repairs and remodeling takes place. Can you see already how important a team is to your success?

Lender

You need at least two lenders: a private money lender and a conventional one. Before you get too far out of the starting gate, you need to get your financial house in order. You should have a standing application at these lenders, with your tax returns and other required documents ready to go. Your lender will be able to qualify you and issue a preapproval letter to you.

When making an offer on a property, having an approval letter in hand, as well as the ability to close quickly, is music to a seller's ears. You want full confidence that whatever you want to buy and finance is not going to be an issue.

Being loyal to a lender, as well as any service provider for that matter, means you can get these services at a discount. A regular customer can have certain lender fees waived or an agent will charge less commission when listing your properties.

Home Inspector

Your home inspector is typically not your contractor, although that's sometimes the case. The contractor will quote and fix what's needed, but it's the inspector who will physically examine the entire property looking for potential issues.

The inspector will see that same crack above the door jamb and notice that the door doesn't shut very well. The inspector will then suggest contacting an engineer, who will visit the property to see if there are any foundation issues.

The inspector will flip light switches, run the sink disposal and cycle the dishwasher and the trash compactor. The basement will be thoroughly reviewed, the attic will be crawled and faucets checked for leaks.

Professional home inspectors use a checklist with hundreds of items that will be checked, including electrical, plumbing and structural, as well as all the appliances to be conveyed. Each item will be marked as "in working order," "needs attention" or "needs replacing."

The inspector will also look for any signs of pest infestation, including wood-destroying insects such as termites or carpenter ants. If there are indications of current or previous problems with termites it will be indicated on the report and a licensed termite inspector will be called. A termite inspection is an option in most places, but in other areas a termite report is a requirement for anyone financing a home.

The home-inspection report will then be presented to you for review, highlighting any items that demand attention. From that report, you will work with your contractor to determine how much the suggested and required repairs will cost.

If the home is actively listed for sale by the owner and the owner's agent, there is an optional form the owner can complete called the Seller's Property Disclosure Statement. This report is similar to the checklist a home inspector might use. The owner is prompted to list any known problems with the property, satisfying the owner's legal requirement to disclose any known defects.

This Disclosure Statement gives you and your inspector a head start. The owner is now aware that he is liable for any non-disclosed problems that he knew about or should have known about. Hiding information of a material nature could result in the seller being held liable for damages.

Title Work

Your contractor and home inspector will help find physical defects, but your title agent or attorney can help you find title defects. Title defects are the unsatisfied liens that appear on the preliminary title report we discussed back in Chapter 5. Depending upon where the property is located, you will order a title report directly from the title agency or through an attorney who will handle your closing.

Recall that if there are certain title issues, you may be inheriting some problems you'd rather not have. In fact, if a seller accepts your offer the property won't be able to transfer to you unless the problems are resolved. A contractor may have performed some work on the home but never got paid.

Without that contractor's mechanic's lien being released, you won't take possession of the property until the lien is cleared and your lender won't finance the purchase. Property tax liens and IRS liens, as well as existing mortgage loans, must be resolved. Without knowing what's on the title, you won't be aware of problems that you can't see. That's before a foreclosure filing has taken place.

Now say that the home has been foreclosed upon by the lender and you attend the auction. The minimum bid required is typically the amount owed to the lender plus associated interest charges, penalties and legal fees.

A foreclosure may wipe out a mechanic's lien or a judgment from the property, but won't release the original owner from the debt. But that's the seller's problem, not yours. However, if there are property tax and IRS liens, they must be paid first before the mortgage is paid off.

A title report can also give you an idea of the owner's current financial condition. Say the home is not yet in foreclosure and you're considering a short sale offer. By looking at the title report, you will see if there are additional liens that must be satisfied, and it will also give you an idea about the potential physical condition of the home. Borrowers who are having problems paying the mortgage will also have problems taking care of home-maintenance issues.

Appraiser

A property appraiser is a licensed professional who makes a determination of a property's current value and an "as completed" value of a potential project. Your real estate agent will provide you with current and future estimated values, but a property appraisal is the report a lender uses when finalizing a value as well as a loan amount.

When a lender orders an appraisal on a property, the lender forwards a copy of the sales contract. The appraiser begins research by accessing county records as well as the local MLS. The appraiser looks for recent home sales that have occurred in the area of similar properties. The appraiser will identify at least three recent sales that have been recorded, and will compare them with the subject property's contract price.

The basic approach compares a price per square foot of comparable homes to the subject property. In addition, the appraiser makes various adjustments that will add or detract from the value of the home. Perhaps the subject property has a larger lot and a view of the mountains, which will add value. Once all the adjustments are made, the final appraised value is issued.

An appraiser on your team can provide you with a more detailed assessment of a property's value based upon sold properties, and should be used when a more formal determination of a project's viability is needed.

Coach

Finally, you should have a coach. A mentor, if you will. Someone who has already blazed a successful trail, and who you can contact when you have a question about real estate financing. Someone you feel comfortable asking any question, and who can act as a backboard when you have an idea.

A mentor is someone who is willing to share knowledge accrued over the years with you to help you avoid potential problems. This book is a form of mentorship, but a true mentor is someone you can contact about a specific scenario or just to get a bit of sage advice.

A mentor is often someone who is currently active in the real estate market, and may be someone to align with as you begin your real estate investing career.

Where can you find a mentor? You can start by visiting a local real estate investment club. You'll find several investors there. If you're brand new, spread the word around that you're willing to help out in any capacity as you learn the industry.

Why would someone become a mentor to you? Because mentors are good people. They're the ones who help because people need help, and they are a rare commodity indeed. Should you find a mentor or a coach, cherish the opportunity and pay it forward as your career progresses. Later on, become a mentor to someone else and teach them what you know. You may not get paid financially as a result of helping someone else start out, but you will be rewarded in ways that truly count.

CHAPTER 9
Protecting Your Assets

When you first start out as a real estate investor you'll likely start out as nothing more than a sole proprietorship. A sole proprietorship is often referred to simply as a "mom and pop" organization because there is no separate legal business entity established. In this chapter we'll talk about the different types of legal business entities and the advantages of each. At this stage, all you may have done is file a "Fictitious Name" document at the county recorder's office, which allows you to legally operate under a business name. There are five basic entities for you to consider:

- Sole Proprietorship
- Limited Liability Company, or LLC
- Limited Partnership, or LP
- General Partnership
- Corporation

What follows is a general description only and is not to be considered as legal advice. I encourage you to speak with an attorney for further details as you move forward in your real estate career.

Sole Proprietorship

A sole proprietorship is a business formation that allows you to operate under a business name while performing business activity as an individual. Your income from a sole proprietorship is listed on your personal income tax return on Schedule C. Income tax is then levied on the net proceeds of the business.

Income tax and real estate investments can take up an entire course on the tax advantages for real estate investors. Rental properties provide multiple opportunities for tax deductions and write-offs, another major appeal that you'll discover.

With a sole proprietorship you will be held personally liable for anything you do on behalf of the company. Both your successes and your failures. If your company is held liable for any damages or claims, it's possible that your personal assets are at risk of being seized should you be on the wrong end of a lawsuit.

For example, say that you're taking an investor to look at a property you're wholesaling along in your car. You have an auto accident along the way, albeit a slight one, but it's your fault. You can't protect yourself using your business as a shield. You are personally liable for any damage beyond what your business can provide.

Limited Liability Company, or LLC

An LLC is the most common entity due to its advantages, as well as the ease of setting one up. An LLC operates just like a corporation, which is a separate legal entity. The LLC is held solely responsible for all business-related activity. Any actions you take as a business owner separate you personally from business operations.

Consider that unfortunate fender bender. Under a sole proprietorship, if your business didn't have enough assets or insurance to settle a claim, your personal insurance policy and assets are at risk. With an LLC, the risk stops at the business, keeping your personal assets free from claims. Income from an LLC is "passed through" directly to the shareholders and taxed once at the individual level.

Limited Partnerships, or LP

A limited partnership, or LP, has a general partner that runs the business — in this instance you. The other partners in the business only risk the amount of capital used to finance the operation and are not liable for any actions the general partner takes during the course of the business. A limited partner simply provides the funds and is not typically involved in day-to-day operations.

The only thing a limited partner risks is the capital, and is protected against legal claims filed against the company. Income is taxed at the individual level as income is passed directly through the partnership to the individual partner.

General Partnership

A general partnership is a legal entity in which several individuals contribute time, talent or capital to run the business. All profits are distributed to the various partners based upon the amount of their cumulative investment and share of the company. Income is also passed through to each individual partner based upon the share of ownership.

Corporation

A corporation is not the typical business model for a small business. A corporation is a separate legal entity from the owners, and protects the investors from any legal liability as a result of day-to-day business activities.

Corporations require a board of directors, annual meetings and minutes taken and recorded at these events. The time and paperwork involved make a corporation last on the list of business entity filings. The LLC provides what a corporation provides in terms of liability and is much less expensive to form as well as maintain.

Now let's look at how trusts operate and when and why you should consider forming one.

Trusts

When setting up a trust, you need the advice and expertise of a trust attorney, but basically there are two types of trusts: revocable and irrevocable.

As you form a trust, you're not necessarily running your business as a trust, although that may be an option for you. A trust is established as a place to transfer your real estate holdings and protect them from outside claims. Once you place a property into a trust, it's nearly impossible for someone to find out where they are. It's as if you put your real estate in a safe.

A revocable trust means it can be changed; an irrevocable trust means it may not. A trust describes the assets being protected and the names of the heirs that will one day receive ownership. The trustee, typically you, is the individual responsible for making sure the instructions in the trust are followed to the letter. Once the trust is legally established, only a revocable trust can make changes.

For example, let's say you have four single-family homes and a nice duplex in the trust, with your daughter and son-in-law as the sole heirs. Once you pass, the property is transferred to them as instructed by the trust. Later, though, the son-in-law turns out to be a jerk and your daughter divorces him. A revocable trust allows the trustee to take the son-in-law off the trust at will.

Insurance

Your first protection against legal claims is your insurance policy. As a sole proprietorship, your personal policy will be your initial line of defense. But liability insurance for those just starting out in the real estate investing world may be an afterthought. If all your real estate activity involves wholesaling, then your business activities that might cause someone to file a claim against you will be limited.

However, if your business involves buying foreclosures, fixing them up and then selling for a profit or holding for long-term appreciation and cash flow, there are additional protections you need to discuss with your insurance agent.

For example, when you're rehabilitating a home or building a brand-new rental from the ground up, you'll need a builder's risk policy. Such a policy covers damages from environmental hazards such as wind, rain and fire, as well as covering any theft of tools, materials and equipment during construction or a remodel. Some homeowner's policies cover property during a remodel; others do not.

As your real estate activities grow, so can your potential liability. Not only will you need to protect your property from damage with a hazard insurance policy; you'll also need to protect it against any legal claims. For example, you have a rental property and your tenants have a party there. A guest shows up and, unfamiliar with the home, slips and falls on some moss-covered rocks. You could be sued. Unfortunately, we live in an extremely litigious society. It's no wonder there are so many legal ads on the radio and TV encouraging listeners to sue for this or make a claim for that.

An annual review with your insurance agent should be on your list to make sure you're covered for property damage as well as any personal or business liability.

CHAPTER 10
The Next Step

So here we are. You're ready to go out and conquer the world. You've made the commitment to be successful investing in real estate and securing your financial future for you and your loved ones. Real estate investing can make you as much money as you want to make, but you do have to work at it.

Everything worth having takes dedication and motivation. You have the tools necessary to be a successful real estate investor so it's time to go, right? Sure, but if you don't know where you're going, how do you know how to get there?

That may be a bit cryptic, but it all boils down to setting goals for you and your business. You may want to make $250,000 this year, but how will you get there? Desire alone is not enough. Yes, you need to have a positive frame of mind and be confident that you can get where you want to go, but positive thinking alone means little. You have to combine that positive attitude with action in order to reach your goals. Let's talk about how to get where you want to go.

Set Your Target

I mentioned making $250,000 in one year. You can do it. Anyone can do it with the right mindset. But how are you going to accomplish that goal, and when? Are you going to flip ten houses and make $25,000 on each one? And if so, when? And if you know when, which property?

This may sound a bit too detailed, but it's how you should begin your goal-setting. After all, if you're planning a trip you don't just fire up the old automobile and start driving, do you? Of course not. You first decide where you want to go, when you're going to leave and how long it will take to get there. If you're old school like me you'll use a map before taking a road trip, with perhaps a little help from a GPS.

Say that you're going to drive from Phoenix to Miami. You look at the map and see that it's pretty much a straight shot: you hop onto Interstate 10, and then head south on Interstate 75. After a couple thousand miles or so you're there.

Yet in between you'll make more than a few pit stops, get fuel, sleep in a hotel and then start all over again. Thirty-six hours of driving time means you'll have to make some basic decisions along the way. But you know where you're going and how you're going to get there.

That's how you set your goals. You can have one major goal, and then intermittent ones that will let you know you're on the right track. There is no shortage of goal-setting books, but they all boil down to a few basic steps.

Write it down. Write down on a pad what you're going to achieve and how you're going to achieve it. This is important. Don't just think about your goals; you need to physically write your goals on your notepad. There's a mental connection that's made when you write your goals down with pen in hand. It's a reinforcement as well as an affirmation.

Next, how are you going to get there? Be as literal as you can. Say you want to close your first deal within ninety days, how are you going to do that? Perhaps you don't have a specific profit requirement for your first transaction—you just want to get the initial one under your belt. What will you do, and when?

- Contact your agent
- Contact your lender
- Find the property by ___
- Close by ___

Ninety days is a relatively short period of time, so you need to constantly keep track of your progress. If something goes awry and your goals need to be adjusted, so be it. Every road trip holds the possibility of an unexpected detour, right? If you need to adjust your goals, go ahead, but don't let that disappoint you. This industry is always changing due to market conditions or regulations, and even the whims of a seller. You need to adapt, but always keep your goals in front of you.

That's the short-term goal. What is your long-term goal? Where do you want to be in one year? Five years? Ten years? Again, write them down. And don't just write them down and throw them in a desk drawer. Keep your goals in front of you where you can see them every day. You will soon find that your actions will automatically achieve those goals as you're constantly reminded of them.

Keep your goals positive. Instead of writing "Don't buy a bad deal" on your notepad, write "Thoroughly and successfully evaluate each project to ensure a profitable outcome!"

Your intermittent goals should be achievable and incremental. Don't concentrate solely on the final outcome; pay attention to the steps needed to get where you want to go. By following the path you've laid down for yourself, you will soon get where you want to be, but you have to pay attention to your process. Remember the old saying about how to eat an elephant: one bite at a time.

It's okay to be nervous at first. When you buy your first property you'll lose that apprehension. I know you will. Heck, today it's easier for me to buy a $200,000 house than it is a $20,000 car. But if you recognize that fear head-on and overcome it, it vanishes because you know you conquered it.

I used to have a fear of public speaking. If you told me years ago that I would be standing in front of hundreds of people giving a speech I would have thought you were nuts, and I know when and where that fear first took hold: in the eighth grade, back in Bedford Hills, New York.

I was scheduled to give an oral presentation in class. I got up in front of my classmates and completely froze. I could not remember a single thing. Not only did my mind go blank, I had no idea what I was talking about. From that point on, every time it was my turn to give a speech in class I would "catch a cold" and stay home. That phobia stayed with me for many years, but today I'm able to comfortably speak in front of any crowd. I faced my fear, and you can too.

Running Your Own Business

Business management covers a wide swath of applications. You can spend four years at a university and get a degree in business management. You don't need to do that, but there are some things that I've learned that can help you as you grow your own company.

First, how big do you want to be? Do you want to be at the top of the mountain and close ten thousand transactions? No? That's perfectly fine—be what you want to be and not what you think others expect you to be. Only you know who you are. Sadly, too many people spend their lives trying to emulate someone that they're really not, and at the end of the day they find they've spent all their time trying to please others at the expense of their own happiness.

You may not want to close ten thousand deals. You may be just fine with owning a few rental properties, living off the cash flow and having something to give your children and your children's children.

I knew at a very early age what my talents were, and even though I may have strayed a few times I never lost sight of who I am and what my skill sets are. My job is to provide people with what they want. I find buyers and I find real estate. Remember that, as a kid, I did pretty well with my lunch money. I'm still using those skills today.

But you need to set your own goals and run at the pace you want to run, not for the expectations of others. Are there things you don't want to do but must? Then farm them out to others. If there's any secret to running a business it might be that—delegate. And at the same time, appreciate the talents of others and nurture them. Don't always force someone to do things your way.   A friend who ran a mortgage company had started out much like me or anyone else, from the ground up. He was good at what he did and soon worked his way up through the company, and was ultimately promoted to vice president. One of his jobs was to generate more loans, which he was very good at. He networked with real estate agents and accountants to establish a respectable book of business.

His company hired a new loan officer and it was his job to train him. So my friend laid out a plan to get loans in the door and told him to visit certain real estate offices and CPAs and establish a working relationship.

But over the next several months, the new loan officer barely brought in any business and his boss was mad at him. He wanted to fire him. He didn't have to because the loan officer quit and went to work with another bank.

A few months later my friend found out that the loan officer was the top producer at his new job, and he surmised that he had finally taken his advice and began calling on real estate agents. My friend wished he would have taken his advice sooner and produced for his mortgage company instead of the other bank.

So one day he called a colleague at the bank and eventually the loan officer's name came up. And he discovered the reason for the loan officer's success: he avoided real estate agents altogether.

You see, he was a bit shy and didn't have the skills needed to make cold calls. It made him uncomfortable and he avoided making sales calls like the plague. Some salesperson, right? But what he did have was an extensive network of friends and colleagues in his alumni association and his church. In fact, he was the president of the alumni association of a rather prestigious university in southern California. He didn't need to make sales calls. All he had to do was let his network know where he worked.

Instead of hiring people to do things a certain way—your way—discover their individual talents and see how they can apply to your business. Let them discover their strong suit and nurture them, don't pigeonhole them.

And finally, be disciplined. Being self-employed is a double-edged sword. You're your own boss and you can set your own hours, but that also means you're your own boss and you can set your own hours.

When working for someone else, you typically have to show up at a specific time, work on specific days and complete specific tasks. In exchange you get paid for your efforts on the first and fifteenth of every month.

You need to have the same sort of discipline when you're on your own. There's no one there to make you get out of bed, go to a meeting or look at a property. You have to do it on your own.

Set a specific time to start work. Get into a routine and treat your business the same as you would if you were working somewhere else five days a week.

You have more flexibility working for yourself, but if you don't treat that flexibility with respect you'll find your success lacking. Face it: some people just aren't made to be self-employed. They need the forced discipline that comes with a "regular" job. That's obviously not you, because you're reading this book. But get into a standard business routine, adjust when needed and get to work. And you know what? You'll soon find out that you're working longer hours than ever before and loving every minute of it.

Getting Social

It's time to move. Get the basics out of the way. Get your website up and running and start marketing your business. If you've never had your own website you might think it's some secret, technical, only-nerds-know-how-to-do-this sort of thing. While that was true several years ago, building a website today could-n't be easier.

There are companies that allow you to register your own website (domain) name and customize a new site using an array of hundreds of website templates.

You can literally log on to any of these internet sites and have your website up and running within an hour or two. All you need to do is input your personal information and write some content about you and your company. And you can do all of this for less than $50.

Think social media is for kids? You've never tweeted? Don't have a Facebook page? It's time to learn. But again, if a twelve-year-old can create a Facebook page, you can. And it's a cheap, easy way to get your name out. Facebook, for example, lets you have a personal page, and then you can create a page for your business.

LinkedIn is considered the "business" version of social media, and you need your presence there, too. As you build your network, each time you reach out and make a post more and more people will receive your message.

Social media isn't a fad; it's another way people and businesses communicate with one another. Still don't have time for social media, or simply don't want to learn? You can hire a social-media manager who can do all of the work for you, from creating your presence to sending out your message.

It's Time to Move

Okay, that's all I can tell you in this book. It's now up to you. There is a lot to learn and you've absorbed a lot of material, but you have the tools you need to get where you want to be. My methods can be used at any time, in any market, anywhere. There doesn't need to be a massive foreclosure wave in order to achieve success, as the principles laid out in this book and in my seminars are real. They're not issued from some theory or possibility, but are honed from real-world experience.

You can do this, you know you can. Welcome to your future, my friend.

—Doug

Glossary

Abstract of Title: A written record of the historical ownership of the property that helps to determine whether the property can in fact be transferred from one party to another without any previous claims. An abstract of title is used in certain parts of the country to determine whether or not there are previous claims on the subject property in question.

Acceleration: A loan accelerates when it is paid off early, usually at the request or demand of the lender. An acceleration clause within a loan document states under what circumstances a loan must be paid immediately. Usually acceleration applies to non-payment, late payments or the transfer of the property without the lender's permission.

Adjustable-Rate Mortgage (ARM): A loan program where the interest rate may change throughout the life of the loan. An ARM adjusts based on terms agreed upon between the lender and the borrower, but typically the interest rate may only change once or twice a year.

Alternate Credit: Items such as your telephone bill, which you must pay each month but which will not appear on your credit report. In relation to mortgage loans, while such items aren't reported as installment or revolving credit, they can establish your ability and willingness to make consistent payments in a responsible manner; also referred to as *nonstandard credit*.

Amortization: A predetermined agreement that stipulates the length of time it takes for a loan to be fully paid off by payments made at regular intervals. Amortization terms can vary, but generally accepted terms run in five-year increments, from ten to forty years; also referred to as a *fully amortized* loan.

Annual Percentage Rate (APR): The cost of money borrowed, expressed as an annual rate. The APR is a useful consumer tool to compare different lenders, but unfortunately, it is often not used correctly. The APR can only work when comparing the exact same loan type from one lender to another.

Appraisable Asset: Any item of which the value can be determined by a third-party expert. For example, your car is an appraisable asset. Funds from items that can be appraised and sold can be used to buy a house.

Appraisal: A report that helps to determine the market value of a property. An appraisal can be done in various ways, as required by a lender, from simply driving by the property to ordering a full-blown inspection, complete with full-color photographs. Appraisals compare similar homes in the area to substantiate the value of the property in question.

Appraisal Management Company (AMS): An independent, third party that receives appraisal orders from lenders or mortgage brokers, which then places the appraisal order and manages the appraisal ordering and receiving process.

APR: *See* Annual Percentage Rate.

ARM: *See* Adjustable Rate Mortgage.

Assumable Mortgage: Homes sold with assumable mortgages let buyers take over the terms of the loan along with the house being sold. Assumable loans may be fully or non-qualifying assumable, meaning buyers take over the loan without being qualified or otherwise evaluated by the original lender. Qualifying assumable loans mean that while buyers may assume terms of the existing note, they must qualify all over again as if they were applying for a brand-new loan.

Automated Valuation Model (AVM): An electronic method of evaluating a property's appraised value; this is done by scanning public records for recent home sales and other data in the subject property's neighborhood. Although not yet widely accepted as a replacement for full-blown appraisals, many in the industry expect AVMs to eventually replace traditional appraisals altogether.

AVM: *See* Automated Valuation Model.

Balloon Mortgage: A type of mortgage in which the remaining balance must be paid in full at the end of a preset term. A five-year balloon mortgage might be amortized over a thirty-year period, but the remaining balance is due, in full, at the end of five years.

Bridge Loan: A short-term loan primarily used to pull equity out of one property for a down payment on another. This loan is paid off when the original property sells. Since they are short-term loans, sometimes lasting just a few weeks, usually only retail banks offer them. Usually the borrower doesn't make any monthly payments, and only pays off the loan when the property sells.

Buydown (permanent and/or temporary): Paying more money to get a lower interest rate is called a *permanent* buydown, and it is used in conjunction with discount points. The more points, the lower the rate. A *temporary* buydown is a fixed-rate mortgage that starts at a reduced rate for the first period, and then gradually increases to its final rate. A temporary buydown for two years is called a 2-1 buydown. For three years it's called a 3-2-1 buydown.

Cash Out: A refinance mortgage that involves taking equity out of a home in the form of cash during a refinance. Instead of just reducing your interest rate during a refinance and financing your closing costs, you finance even more, putting the additional money in your pocket.

Closer: The person who helps to prepare the lender's closing documents. The closer forwards those documents to your settlement agent's office, where you will be signing closing papers. In some states, a closer can be the person who holds your loan.

Closing Costs: The various fees involved during the process of buying a home or obtaining a mortgage. The fees, required to issue a good loan, can come directly from the lender or may come from others in the transactions.

Collateral: Collateral is property owned by the borrower that's pledged to the lender as security in case the loan goes bad. A lender makes a mortgage with the house as collateral.

Comparable Sales: Comparable sales are that part of an appraisal report that lists recent transfers of similar properties in the immediate vicinity of the house being bought; also referred to as *comps*.

Conforming Loan: A conventional conforming loan is a Fannie Mae or Freddie Mac loan, which is equal to or less than the maximum allowable loan limits established by Fannie Mae and Freddie Mac. These limits are changed annually.

Conventional Loan: A mortgage loan that uses guidelines established by Fannie Mae or Freddie Mac and is issued and guaranteed by lenders.

Credit Report: A report that shows the payment histories of a consumer, as well as the individual's property addresses and any public records.

Credit Repository: A place where credit histories are stored. Merchants and banks agree to store consumers' credit patterns in a central place that all merchants and banks can access.

Credit Score: A number derived from a consumer's credit history, and which is based upon various credit details in a consumer's past, and upon the likelihood of default. Different credit patterns are assigned different numbers, and different credit activity may have a greater or lesser impact on the score. The higher the credit score, the better the credit.

Debt Consolidation: Paying off all or part of one's consumer debt with equity from a home. Debt consolidation can be part of a refinanced mortgage or a separate equity loan.

Debt Ratio: Gross monthly payments divided by gross monthly income, expressed as a percentage. There are typically two debt ratios to be considered: 1) The *housing ratio*—sometimes called the *front-end* or *front* ratio—is the total monthly house payment, plus any monthly tax, insurance, private mortgage insurance or homeowner's association dues, divided by gross monthly income. 2) The *total debt ratio*—also called the *back-end* or *back* ratio—is the total housing payment plus other monthly consumer installment or revolving debt, also expressed as a percentage. Loan–debt ratio guidelines are usually denoted as 32/38, with 32 being the front ratio and the 38 being the back ratio. Ratio guidelines can vary from loan to loan and lender to lender.

Deed: A written document proving every transfer of ownership in a property.

Deed in Lieu: An abbreviated term for *deed in lieu of a foreclosure*. A deed in lieu is initiated and carried out by the borrower, who transfers all interest in the subject property to the lender.

Deed of Trust: A written document giving an interest in the home being bought to a third party, usually the lender, as security to the lender.

Delinquent: Being behind on a mortgage payment. Delinquencies typically begin to be recognized as 30+ days delinquent, 60+ days delinquent and 90+ days delinquent.

Discount Points: Also called *points*, discount points are represented as a percentage of a loan amount. One point equals one percent of a loan balance. Borrowers pay discount points to reduce the interest rate for a mortgage. Typically each discount point paid reduces the interest rate by a quarter of one percent. It is a form of prepaid interest to a lender.

Document Stamp: Evidence—usually with an ink stamp—of how much tax was paid upon transfer of ownership of property. Certain states call it a *doc stamp.* Doc stamp tax rates can vary based upon locale, and not all states have doc stamps.

Down Payment: The amount of money initially given by the borrower to close a mortgage. The down payment equals the sales price less financing. It's the very first bit of equity you'll have in your new home.

Easement: A right of way previously established by a third party. Easement types can vary but typically involve the right of a public utility to cross your land to access an electrical line.

Equity: The difference between the appraised value of a home and any outstanding loans recorded against the house.

Escrow: Depending upon where you live, escrow can mean two things. On the West Coast, for example, when a home goes under contract it *goes into escrow* (*see also* Escrow Agent). In other parts of the country, an escrow is a financial account set up by a lender to collect monthly installments for annual tax bills and/or hazard insurance policy renewals.

Escrow Account: *See* Impound Account.

Escrow Agent: On the West Coast, the escrow agent is the person or company that handles the home closing, ensuring that documents are assigned correctly and property transfer has legitimately changed hands.

FACTA: *See* Fair and Accurate Credit Transactions Act.

Fair and Accurate Credit Transactions Act (FACTA): A new law that replaces the Fair Credit Reporting Act, or FCRA, and governs how consumer information can be stored, shared and monitored for privacy and accuracy.

Fair Credit Reporting Act (FCRA): The first consumer law that emphasized consumer rights and protections relating to their credit reports, their credit applications and privacy concerns.

Fannie Mae: *See* Federal National Mortgage Association.

FCRA: *See* Fair Credit Reporting Act.

Federal Home Loan Mortgage Corporation: The FHLMC, or Freddie Mac, is a corporation established by the U.S. government in 1968 to buy mortgages from lenders made under Freddie Mac guidelines.

Federal Housing Administration (FHA): Now a division of the Federal Housing Finance Agency, the FHA was formed in 1934 and provides loan guarantees to lenders who make loans under FHA guidelines.

Federal Housing Finance Agency (FHFA): Established as the result of the Housing and Economic Recovery Act of 2008, this agency controls Fannie Mae, Freddie Mac, HUD and the Federal Home Loan Banks.

Federal National Mortgage Association: The FNMA, or Fannie Mae, was originally established in 1938 by the U.S. government to buy FHA mortgages and provide liquidity in the mortgage marketplace. It is similar in function to Freddie Mac. In 1968, the Fannie Mae charter was changed and the association now purchases conventional mortgages as well as government ones.

Federal Reserve Board: The head of the Federal Reserve Banks that, among other things, sets overnight lending rates for banking institutions. Also known as *The Fed*, the Federal Reserve Board does not set mortgage rates.

Fed Funds Rate: The rate banks charge one another to borrow money overnight.

Fed: Shorthand name for the Federal Reserve Board.

FHA: *See* Federal Housing Administration.

FICO: *See* Fair Isaac Corporation.

Fair Isaac Corporation (FICO): The company that invented the most widely used credit scoring system.

Final Inspection: The last inspection of a property, which verifies that a newly built home is 100 percent complete or that a home-improvement project is 100 percent complete. Final inspection lets lenders know that their collateral and their loan are exactly where they should be.

Fixed Rate Mortgage: A loan whose interest rate does not change throughout the term of the loan.

Flood Certificate: A certificate that shows whether a property or part of a property lies above or below any local flood zones. These flood zones are mapped over the course of several years by the Federal Emergency Management Agency (FEMA). The certificate identifies the property's exact legal location and a flood line's elevation. There is a box that simply asks, "Is the property in a flood zone, yes or no?" If the property is in a flood zone, the lender will require special flood insurance that is not usually carried under a standard homeowner's hazard insurance policy.

Foreclosure: An unfortunate event that happens when the mortgage isn't repaid. Lenders begin the process of forcefully recovering their collateral when borrowers fail to make loan payments. In short, the lender takes the house away.

Freddie Mac: *See* Federal Home Loan Mortgage Corporation.

Gift: When the down payment and closing costs for a home are given to the borrower instead of the funds coming from their own accounts. Usually such gifts can only come from family members or foundations established to help new homeowners.

Gift Affidavit: A form signed whereby someone swears that the money they're giving you is indeed a gift, not a loan, and is to be used for the purchase of a home. Lenders like to see that form, as well as a paper trail of the gift funds being added to the borrowers own funds.

Gift Funds: Monies given to a borrower for the sole purpose of buying a home. These funds are not to be paid back in any form and are usually given by a family member or a qualified non-profit organization.

Government National Mortgage Association: The GNMA, or Ginnie Mae, is a U.S. government corporation formed to purchase government loans like Veterans Affairs (VA) and FHA loans from banks and mortgage lenders.

Good Faith Estimate: A list of estimated closing costs on a particular mortgage transaction. This estimate must be provided to the loan applicants within three business days after receipt of a mortgage application by the lender or broker.

Hazard Insurance: A specific type of insurance that covers against certain destructive elements such as fire, wind and hail. It is usually an addition to homeowners insurance, but every home loan has a hazard rider.

HELOC: *See* Home Equity Line of Credit.

Home Equity Line of Credit (HELOC): A credit line that uses a home as collateral. Customers write checks on this line of credit whenever they need to, and pay only on balances withdrawn. A HELOC is much like a credit card, but secured by the property.

Homeowners Insurance: An insurance policy that covers not just hazard items, but also other things, such as liability or personal property.

Home Valuation Code of Conduct (HVCC): Established as a national lending rule that prohibits lenders or mortgage brokers from influencing property values by communicating directly with an appraiser; HVCC provides rules for ordering, compensating and selecting an appraiser.

Impound Account: An account that is set up by a lender to deposit a monthly portion of annual property taxes or hazard insurance. As taxes or insurance come up for renewal, the lender pays the bill using these funds. Also referred to as an *escrow account.*

Inspection: A structural review of the house to determine defects in workmanship, damage to the property or required maintenance. An inspection does not determine value of the property. A pest inspection, for example, looks for termites or wood ants.

Installment Account: Borrowing one lump sum and agreeing to pay back a certain amount each month until the loan is paid off. A car loan is an example of an installment loan.

Interest Rate: The amount charged to borrowed money over a specified period of time.

Interest Rate Reduction Loan (IRRL): A Veterans Affairs (VA) refinance loan program that has relaxed credit guidelines. Also referred to as a *streamline refinance*.

IRRL: *See* Interest Rate Reduction Loan.

Jumbo Loan: A mortgage that exceeds current conforming loan limits.

Junior Lien: A second mortgage or one that subordinates to another loan. Not as common a term as it used to be. You're more likely to hear the terms *second mortgage* or *piggyback.*

Land Contract: An arrangement in which the buyer makes monthly payments to the seller but the ownership of the property does not change hands until the loan is paid in full.

Land-to-Value: An appraisal term that calculates the value of the land as a percentage of the total value of the home. If the land exceeds the value of the home it's more difficult to find financing without good comparable sales. Also referred to as *lot-to-value*.

Lease-Purchase Agreement: An option whereby a buyer leases a home until the buyer has saved up enough money for a down payment to qualify for a conventional mortgage; also referred to as *rent-to-own*.

Lender Policy: Title insurance that protects a mortgage from defects or previous claims of ownership.

Liability: An obligation or bill on the part of the borrower. It works like an automobile loan. When you pay off the car, you get the title. Liabilities such as student loans or a car payment can show up on a credit report, but they can also be anything else that you are obligated to pay. Those liabilities on the credit report are used to determine debt ratios.

Lien: A legal claim or prior interest on the property you're about to buy. Borrowing money from another source in order to buy a house could mean that someone else has a lien on that property.

Loan: Money granted to one party with the expectation that the money will be repaid.

Loan Originator: The person who is typically responsible for helping mortgage applicants become qualified for a loan, and who assists in loan selection and loan application. Loan originators can work at banks, credit unions, and mortgage brokerage houses or for bankers.

Loan Processor: The person who gathers the required documentation for a loan application and for loan submission. Along with a loan originator, borrowers will work with the loan processor quite a bit during the mortgage process.

Loan Underwriter: The person responsible for ultimately saying *yes* or *no* on a loan file. The underwriter compares loan guidelines with what you have documented in the file.

Loan-to-Value Ratio (LTV): A ratio expressed as a percentage of the loan amount when compared to the valuation of the home determined by an appraisal. If a home was appraised at $100,000 and the loan amount was $70,000, then the LTV would be 70 percent.

LTV: *See* Loan-to-Value Ratio.

Market Value: In an open market, the market value of a property is both the highest the borrower is willing to pay and the least the seller is willing to accept at the time of contract. Property appraisals help justify market value by comparing similar home sales in the subject property's neighborhood.

Mortgage: A loan with the property being pledged as collateral. The mortgage is retired when the loan is paid in full.

Mortgage Brokers: Companies that set up a home loan between a banker and a borrower. Similar to how an independent insurance agent operates, brokers don't have money to lend directly, but they have experience in finding various loan programs that can suit the borrower. Brokers don't work for the borrower but instead provide mortgage loan choices from other mortgage lenders.

Mortgagee: The person or business making the loan; also referred to as *the lender*.

Mortgagor: The person(s) getting the loan; also referred to as *the borrower*.

Multiple Listing Service (MLS): A central repository where real estate brokers and agents show homes and search for homes that are for sale.

Nonconforming: Loans whose amounts are above current Fannie Mae or Freddie Mac limits. *See also* Jumbo Loan.

Note: A promise to repay. It may or may not have property involved and it may or may not be a mortgage.

Note Modification: A process whereby a mortgage lender modifies the current structure of the outstanding note, often to assist a borrower who may be having difficulties making their regular mortgage payment as reflected by the original note.

Notice of Default (NOD): Delivered by certified letter from the mortgage lender to the borrower when two successive mortgage payments have been missed. A legal process filing, the NOD becomes a public record, recorded in the county or parish where the property resides.

Origination Fee: A fee charged to cover costs associated with finding, documenting and preparing a mortgage application, and usually expressed as a percentage of the loan amount.

Owner's Policy: Title insurance made for the benefit of the homeowner.

Payment Shock: A term used by lenders referring to the percentage difference between what you're paying now for housing and what your new payment would be. Most loan programs don't have a payment shock provision, but for those that do, a common percentage increase is 150 percent.

Principal, Interest, Taxes and Insurance (PITI): These figures are used to help determine front debt ratios. In condos, townhouses or co-ops homeowner's association dues replace the payment for insurance.

Portfolio Loan: A loan made by a direct lender, usually a bank, and kept in the lender's loan portfolio instead of being sold or underwritten to any external guidelines.

Pre-foreclosure: A property where foreclosure is imminent; often associated with an impending or current Notice of Default (NOD).

Prepaid Interest: Daily interest collected from the day of loan closing to the first of the following month.

Principal: The outstanding amount owed on a loan, not including any interest due.

Private Lender: An individual or group of individuals who finance real estate using their own terms and their own funds. Primarily used to finance transactions that banks typically refuse to finance.

Quit Claim: A release of any interest in a property from one party to another. A quit claim does not, however, release the obligation on the mortgage.

Rate-and-Term Refinance: Refinancing to get a new rate. The process includes changing the interest rate and changing the term, or length, of the new note. Refinancing requires a full approval process exactly as the purchase loan was issued.

Realtor: A member of the *National Association of Realtors* and a registered trademark. Not all real estate agents are realtors.

Recast: A term applied to ARMs and used when extra payments are made to the principal balance. When your note is recast, your monthly payment is calculated for you.

Refinance: Obtaining a new mortgage to replace an existing one. There is also a *rate-and-term refinance*, in which only the outstanding principal balance, interest due and closing costs are included in the loan.

Reissue: When refinancing, there may be discounts if you use the same title agency. Reissue of an original title report can cost much less than a full title insurance policy.

Rescission: To withdraw or *rescind* from a mortgage agreement. Refinanced mortgage loans for a primary residence have a required three-day *cooling off* period before the loan becomes official. If for any reason you decide not to take the mortgage, you can rescind and the whole deal's off.

Reserves: A borrower's assets after closing. Reserves can include cash in the bank, stocks, mutual funds, retirement accounts, IRAs and 401(k) accounts.

WINNING THE PROPERTY WAR

Revolving Account: A credit card or department store account on which you typically have a credit limit and on which you make no payments until you charge something.

Sales Contract: A written agreement to sell or purchase a home, signed by both the seller and buyer.

Second Mortgage: Sometimes called a *piggyback mortgage*, a second mortgage assumes a subordinate position behind a first mortgage. If the home goes into foreclosure, the first mortgage would be settled before the second could lay claim. *See also* Junior Lien.

Seller: The person transferring ownership and all rights for a home in exchange for cash or trade.

Settlement Statement: Also called the Final HUD-1, this statement shows all financial entries during the home sale, including sales price, closing costs, loan amounts and property taxes. Your initial good faith estimate will be your first glimpse of your settlement statement. This statement is one of the final documents put together before you go to closing and is prepared by your attorney or settlement agent.

Short Sale: When a property changes hands from seller to buyer, the lender has agreed to accept less for their outstanding mortgage note than the current balance or payoff amount and the seller is released from all future obligation to repay the mortgage and any delinquent amounts.

Survey: A map that shows the physical location of a structure (e.g., a house) and where it sits on the property. A survey also designates any easements that run across or through the property.

Title Insurance: Protection for the lender, the seller and/or the borrower against any defects or previous claims to the property being transferred or sold.

Title: A document showing legal ownership in a property.

Title Exam/Title Search: The process whereby public records are reviewed to research any previous liens on the property.

Trust Deed Sale: In states where trust deeds are used to transfer property, a trust deed sale is an auction where investors bid against one another to buy a foreclosed property.

Underwater Mortgage: A term used to describe a piece of leveraged real estate where the mortgage balance exceeds the current property value.

Veterans Affairs (VA) Loan: Government mortgage guaranteed by the Department of Veterans Affairs.

VA No-No: A type of VA loan where the borrower not only puts *no* money down, but also pays *no* closing costs.

Verification of Deposit (VOD): A form mailed to a bank or credit union that asks the institution to verify that a borrower's bank account exists, how much money is in the account, how long the borrower has had the account and what the average balance was over the previous two months.

VOD: *See* Verification of Deposit.

Wholesaling: Agreeing to purchase a property for one price, and then assigning the rights to purchase to a third party for a profit.

Wrap-Around Mortgage: A method of financing in which the borrower pays the former owner of the property each month in the form of a mortgage payment. The former owner will then make a mortgage payment to the original mortgage holder. This kind of mortgage is not allowed without initial lender's permission.